I0754771

Handbook for the Revolution

Building a More Perfect Union

Handbook for the Revolution

DERRICK PALMER

for the Twenty-First Century

AUWA BOOKS
MCD / Farrar, Straus and Giroux
New York

AUWA Books
MCD / Farrar, Straus and Giroux
120 Broadway, New York 10271

EU Representative: Macmillan Publishers Ireland Ltd, 1st Floor, The Liffey Trust Centre, 117–126 Sheriff Street Upper, Dublin 1, D01 YC43

Printed in the United States of America
First edition, 2026

Library of Congress Control Number: 2026931334
ISBN: 978-0-374-61371-6

Designed by Gretchen Achilles

10 9 8 7 6 5 4 3 2 1

To my mother, who's been there for me
for my entire journey in life.

And to the hardworking organizers and
soon-to-be organizers across the world.

Contents

5. Playing the Long Game

Handbook for the Revolution

Introduction

On April 1, 2022, my fellow workers and I celebrated a historic victory at JFK8, an Amazon Fulfillment Center warehouse in Staten Island, New York. We voted to unionize, becoming Amazon's first organized facility in the country. Our Amazon Labor Union (ALU) was founded and led by four friends: Christian Smalls, Gerald Bryson, Jordan Flowers, and me. We were independent, upstart, and worker-led. The union was an extension of the Congress of Essential Workers (TCOEW), which we created back when we first walked off the job in March 2020 during the Covid pandemic. Amazon and its cutthroat founder, Jeff Bezos, the second-richest person in the world with a net worth of around $200 billion, were determined that we would fail against his multitrillion-dollar company. But together, we defeated America's second-largest employer, and one of the most powerful corporations on the planet.

Ours is a true David and Goliath story.

It's been a wild ride since then. Chris and I were on *Time* magazine's list of 2022's Most Influential People, were named a "Dynamic Duo" on the 2022 *Ebony* Power 100 list, and received many other honors. After our victory, workers across the country, including at Whole Foods, Starbucks, Target, Walmart, Dollar General, and other companies, have repeatedly reached out to us with the same question: How did we do it? It's a great question. The simple answer is that we learned the hard way, through trial and error. More importantly, we created a whole new playbook that was completely different from the one traditional union organizers have relied on for the past sixty years. Our strategies were fresh, original, and meant to serve today's workforce. The ALU that we created was something America had never seen before.

Now I want to share the story of how the ALU grew and became stronger as a collective team. This book is a manifesto for a rising labor movement that is desperately needed in this country. In it, I share our strategies and tactics, and the ups and downs of being organizers; the good, the bad, and the ugly. My hope is that other activists and union leaders will be inspired by our original yet unorthodox approach and that they won't have to repeat the same mistakes we made, or the same mistakes made by others around us.

This is the book that I wish Chris and I had back in 2021 when we first decided—on a late-night drive home from Bessemer, Alabama—that we would start a union on Staten Island. It's the definitive how-to guide for organizing: a step-by-step introduction to the deeply personal and often painful process of bringing a union to today's workplace.

Throughout the unionizing process and after, one of the biggest surprises, and disappointments, for me has been the realization that not only did we, the founders of the ALU, have to battle Amazon and conservative anti-labor political forces, but we also faced counterattacks from within our own movement. Sometimes these attacks came from a place of jealousy or a desire for power. Sometimes they were also rooted in a kind of unconscious, or maybe conscious, racism. After all, we were four strong Black men who dared to lead a revolutionary movement without asking for permission from anybody, not even from powerful national, traditional unions. I think some people find that reality hard to accept. But we persevered, despite attacks from all sides and constant attempts to dismantle what we had built.

My hope is that I can help prepare other organizers for the many roadblocks and obstacles that lie ahead on their path, both practical and ideological. In this book, I acknowledge and engage with some of the larger societal questions, like why workers still don't have the basic rights that we deserve in this country. At the same time, I also tackle everyday logistical questions like, "How do I know if my workplace needs a union?" and "How do I get authorization cards signed?"

In my case, and in the case of so many organizers, the process of becoming a leader starts with anger, which is not necessarily a bad thing. Sometimes a sense of righteous outrage and indignation is so overpowering that it can't be ignored. We've all felt that breaking point. The circumstances might be different, but we all share that small voice inside that finally says, "No more."

One of the first things I do when I talk to other workers is to share the story of my own breaking point and how it led to a new sense of confidence and empowerment. Whatever our unique experiences may be, I've found that as workers, our end goal is the same: to move from anger to strength. In this book, I hope to help workers discover their own path toward organizing, for themselves.

1.

My Amazon Story: Moving from Angry to Activated

Finding My Voice

Nothing in my life suggested that I would become a labor organizer. Like so many who clock in to a job, I had set out to work hard and to do everything I could to get ahead. What I didn't realize at the time was that I was working within a system that in my opinion had been designed to stop people like me—Black, working-class, without a fancy four-year college degree—from moving up. It took a while, but when I hit that ceiling at Amazon's JFK8 warehouse on Staten Island, I realized that the rights I thought we all had as workers didn't apply equally to everyone. I began to feel disillusioned and angry. I wasn't alone. Many of my coworkers were feeling similar frustrations.

Growing up, I wasn't always a confident person. I was a small kid. Soft-spoken. Walked with my head down at times. Often, my anxieties would get the best of me. But I loved being outside, going to the park, riding my bike, and playing basketball. I loved to make people laugh, and I like to think my heart was in the right place.

I was born in Orange, New Jersey, and spent my first years in nearby Plainfield. My parents divorced when I was a baby, and I was raised by a hardworking single parent named Carol Boulden. My mother and I didn't really stay in touch with my father when I was young, but I was in contact with four siblings on my father's side. When I was five, my mom moved us to Piscataway, New Jersey. I was my mother's only child, and for the most part it was just the two of us, sharing a one-bedroom apartment throughout my childhood and teenage years. Sometimes she would take the bedroom, and sometimes I would.

After I graduated from Piscataway High School in 2007 at age eighteen, I enrolled at Middlesex College in New Jersey, where I planned to major in theater. I had always loved acting and had enjoyed attending theater camp for a few years in middle school, thanks to my mom. Even though I was shy offstage, I discovered that I could break out of my shell when I was performing. I loved to do impersonations and study famous actors to learn more about the craft. For a long time, acting was really what I thought I wanted to do with my life. But I wasn't applying myself to my studies. Instead, I was hanging out with friends, skipping class. When my mom saw I was stalling out, she found a marketing job at a cable company in East Windsor, New Jersey, and we moved there. She thought a different environment might help give me a fresh start.

I transferred to Mercer County Community College in West Windsor in 2008 and gave college another try. I also got a job working part-time as a cashier at a TJ Maxx down the street from my house. But I could feel that I was drifting, and I was still unsure about what to do with my life. I felt unmotivated and without direction. I ended up dropping out a year later in 2009, keeping my job at TJ Maxx. Then, in 2011, at age twenty-one, I left that job to work at the Williams Sonoma warehouse in Cranbury, New Jersey, where I worked ten-hour shifts loading trucks with heavy furniture supplies.

When I was twenty-two, my grandfather died. It was a big blow for all of us. He was a strong leader who always brought our family together. My grandfather was strict and believed in setting goals. In 1945, he was inducted in the U.S. Army and worked his way through the ranks, as a noncommissioned officer (NCO) and as a commissioned officer. He served in both the active army and the reserves for twenty years and retired as a major. I feel like he's part of the reason I became who I am today. He passed that sense of determination down to my mother, and to me, although at the time I didn't see it. That year, I got a tattoo on my arm that said, "RIP Grand-pop." The next year, I got another one with two half faces: one smiling, one sad. It was symbolic. In public, I felt like I was putting up a positive front, but in private I was hurting.

In 2015 I was twenty-five years old and still had not found a clear path. When my mom told me Amazon was hiring at the EWR4 warehouse in Robbinsville, New Jersey, I decided to apply. I submitted my application on Indeed .com and was immediately called in. There was no résumé required. No interview. I guess they didn't plan on having me stay very long, which I later learned was exactly Amazon's plan for hourly warehouse workers. The mentality was to keep a high turnover rate, which some call Bezos's "churn and burn" strategy. At first, I was told that I would be a seasonal, part-time worker, or what we call a "white badge" worker. When I showed up, though, I was told I would be "blue badge," full-time. This was a great thing for me, especially since I knew that many part-time workers didn't receive benefits and were getting laid off after six months.

I worked in the Count department, keeping track of inventory. I was a hard worker, even though it was tough to stand still for ten hours. There was a feeling of isolation, too. But what bothered me most was that over time, I noticed that some of my coworkers who had the same skills, experience, and productivity level that I did were getting promoted and moving ahead while I stayed stuck. I began to get really frustrated. At some point, I told myself that maybe I just needed a new approach.

So, in 2018, I decided to try a different angle. I took a temporary assignment at JFK8, a brand-new Amazon warehouse on Staten Island, where I was sent to work as an ambassador, training new associates. Looking back, this was a key moment for me. I did a three-week "away team" assignment that was exciting and new. Being an ambassador meant you were the first person a new worker would meet. You were their first impression of the company and the person who set the tone for their entire work experience. The way you trained and interacted with them could determine their future.

I thought, "Okay! Now I can really begin to move up." I started talking to everyone who would listen—the general manager, the operations manager, human resources—asking for a permanent transfer to JFK8. It took a little time, but soon, I got what I'd asked for.

When I first took the ambassador assignment, I had no idea that it would involve talking to a crowd. Sometimes I'd have a group of ten new workers staring at me, depending on me to show them the ropes. Given my shyness, that was kind of overwhelming for me at first. Later, there would be as many as sixty or seventy people waiting to hear presentations from me. For example, if the learning trainer, who was above me in rank, wasn't there that day, they'd ask me to do a presentation on something general like hazmat. Suddenly, I had to stand up and speak to even bigger crowds!

I wasn't sure I would be a fit for the role. But as I started meeting and interacting with more workers, I realized that I was good at my job. Really good. I began to see that I had a lot to offer. As I began to overcome my anxiety, I discovered that I had a way of helping people grow and move forward. Given what happened later, it was kind of ironic, if you think about it. Becoming an ambassador at Amazon helped to bring out the leader inside of me that had always been there.

Here's an example of how I was able to help other workers at the time. Amazon had a training manual that, I believe, was mostly useless. It was missing a lot of information and didn't show any of the mistakes that people tend to make. Like, for pickers—the group of workers who retrieve items from bins based on customer orders—guidelines weren't always clear. For example, when an item pops up on the screen at your station, the computer is supposed to tell you which bin to go to so you can find it. But a lot of times, the computer messes up and shows a picture that doesn't match the item's description. None of that was in the training manual. So I put it aside and freestyled my training demonstrations. I explained to new workers that when the computer messed up, you had to check the barcode to find the right bin. These were small nuances that really helped them out.

When I hit my two-year mark at the company, I was able to get around two thousand dollars in Amazon stock, which was a bonus that they used to offer new workers. It came exactly when I needed it. I cashed out and used the money for a down payment on an apartment in Elizabeth, New Jersey, to help shorten my commute to JFK8. The tolls on my commute were still crazy expensive, but it was better than before. It wasn't until years later that I was finally able to move to an apartment on Staten Island, which I now share with a roommate.

After my permanent transfer to JFK8, it didn't take long for me to realize that I already had more experience than most other workers at the company. Ambassadors were usually trained in just one department. So, if you were a picker, you would be an ambassador for only that section. To the best of my knowledge, I was the first person in the warehouse's history to perform and train in multiple roles. I was an ambassador for Pick as well as Count, the department that keeps track of inventory and investigates any discrepancies. And I was good at all the counts: simple record count, simple bin count, cycle count. I also did jam clearing, manually removing items stuck on conveyer belts, and was a process guide, which is a kind of mentoring role. I could do it all, which meant I was saving the company a lot of money.

For five years, I served as an ambassador in addition to my daily job, working hard and giving 100 percent. Along the way, I was told that the work I was doing was a stepping stone to the next level. I believed that doing multiple jobs would qualify me for consideration to become a process assistant and then a learning trainer. It had to! In any other situation, performing all these roles *should* qualify someone to advance, especially since I knew I was one of the best ambassadors Amazon had. I even got a special certificate that they gave out to ambassadors for training new hires during the holiday season. It gave us ten hours of personal time off as a reward, a practice that Amazon stopped doing for ambassadors in 2019. Today, they might still give out small gifts to ambassadors, but it's more like a branded water bottle or a key chain.

Hitting a Wall

I should have been promoted by any objective measure. That was obvious. But in my case, there was a problem. I'll call him John Stanton, a young white guy from South Jersey who was an operations manager in our department. John had a strange energy. We all felt it. Usually someone in his position doesn't work hands-on, on the floor. They typically monitor activities from their computer. But with John, there was a lot of micromanaging going on. He was always checking on us. A lot of the time, he'd come to my station and send me to other locations for no reason.

"They need help downstairs," he'd say. I was overqualified to move up, but instead, all John did was constantly move me around to different entry-level stations. It felt like he wanted to overwork me. This really stirred the pot for me and escalated my frustrations.

Whenever I asked my immediate supervisor about a promotion, she'd say the same thing: "It's out of my hands." I had no idea what the issue was. My performance was solid. Even Amazon said so. Then, I thought, "Maybe the problem is her." So I went to HR and asked them to switch my manager. "I want someone who has my best interests in mind," I said.

That's when I met Chris Smalls. He was a top-performing process assistant, which is kind of like an assistant manager. He had started at Amazon in 2015, like me, and quickly moved up from picker to warehouse associate to process assistant, all in his first year. He'd trained hundreds of employees, including some in management. When he was at BDL2 in Connecticut, he applied unsuccessfully to be a manager forty-nine times. That tells you something about his determination.

We had something else in common, too. Both of us were there in the first place because of our moms. They were the ones who had told us Amazon was hiring and pushed us to apply. It was funny. Chris's mom even pretty much did half of the application for him, he said.

Because of my request for a new manager, I was put on a whole new team. I now was working alongside Chris and a man named Gerald Bryson, who worked in Pick and Robotics. The three of us would later become ALU cofounders along with Jordan Flowers. We all worked for a new direct manager, Bertram Pryce, who was also Black. This made our team unusual. In fact, Bertram was the only Black manager at JFK8.

What was strange about John Stanton was that he kept his eye on me even after my transfer out of his jurisdiction. I found out later that he would specifically ask about me. "What's Derrick doing? What role does he have now?" Once, he told me that he saw me as "the LeBron James of Amazon." Now you can read into that in all kinds of ways. Basically, though, the bottom line was that I feared he was doing me dirty. From the moment I arrived at JFK8 in 2018, already with three years of seniority, I should have been a manager. But I was convinced that John never wanted me to move up.

Bertram was different. He constantly gave me opportunities to grow and learn. Because he saw my potential, I was able to interview for promotions. In my opinion, Bertram was also a victim of Amazon's discrimination, though. He had come to JFK8 at a higher level than many of the white managers because he already had prior experience as an operations manager at Target. In the end, he transferred to an Amazon facility in Brooklyn, where he was finally promoted to operations manager.

Still, even with Bertram's support, the problem of John Stanton never went away. When I interviewed for promotions, I was told that I nailed them. What I didn't realize was that it was operations managers who had to approve all promotions. It didn't matter that Bertram was my direct manager and that he believed in me. John would always be the puppet master who controlled the strings. I later found out that he was the one who constantly instructed people not to consider me as a candidate to move up. It wasn't until many years later that I started to understand why.

Jodi Kantor at *The New York Times* has published a lot of reporting on Amazon. Her 2021 investigations uncovered the fact that there was an unfair system of promotions at Amazon, and that the system was by design. Hires for management and corporate jobs were reserved for college graduates, not warehouse workers, it was revealed. Basically, there was never going to be such a thing as "moving up" for me.

Another *New York Times* report revealed that Amazon's management was more than 70 percent white, while the warehouse workforce at JFK8 was more than 60 percent people of color. It also found that Black workers in our specific building were nearly 50 percent more likely to be fired than white workers. After that report was released, Amazon introduced diversity plans and made a show of trying to recruit more Black managers. They brought in a guy from Alabama, but it turns out that he was just a union buster. By 2025, emboldened by President Donald Trump's anti-DEI backlash, Amazon, along with many other U.S. companies, removed any mention of DEI completely from its goals.

But back then, before the union and all these news reports, I hadn't quite put all the pieces together yet, although I was beginning to have my suspicions. One day, I went directly to the general manager, Chris Colvin, and told him I believed I was being discriminated against and unfairly targeted. I filed a report that specified the cause as racism, which I hand delivered to human resources. When I finally got the chance to meet with Colvin, I was hopeful that he might finally do something about my situation.

I explained everything, and he listened in a way that made it seem like he heard me. But then, as I headed back to my station, I saw John Stanton go into Colvin's office right behind me. I could see them through the glass, looking at each other's phones and acting like old buddies. That's when it hit me. I was in a lose-lose situation. It was a hard realization to take. I was convinced I was never going to move up. It was a realization that would literally change the course of my life.

An Atomic Moment

Racism *is* an issue at Amazon and at so many companies. There's no denying it. Chris Smalls experienced the same kind of micromanaging and gatekeeping. So did Gerald Bryson. So did Bertram Pryce. We all did. We all were met with the same disrespect and disregard, even though we were highly productive. Because of this discrimination, we remained stagnant. My frustrations piled up higher and higher. And if there's one thing that I've learned about worker movements, it's this: In most cases there's a tipping point when we've had enough. It's a moment when there's no longer any hesitation. You feel like you just *have* to do something. We call that an "atomic moment."

At JFK8, ours came in March 2020.

In every Amazon warehouse break room, there are about eight giant-screen TVs, all typically set to the news and sports. But in early March 2020 that changed. As Covid cases shot up and New York City became the center of the worst outbreaks, we found that, strangely, there was no news playing on any of the TVs. In fact, they played literally anything *but* the news. I concluded that the company made a conscious effort to keep us uninformed about the pandemic, the risks, and how we should have been protecting ourselves.

I remember that Chris and I were in the break room one day sitting shoulder to shoulder and joking about how we were going to die because we should have been six feet apart and wearing masks. Amazon had no personal protective equipment (PPE) and no social distancing. Inside the facility it was just business as usual. Or not even business as usual. Business was booming. Because just as the rest of the world was being sent home, Amazon was making door-to-door deliveries. This was their moment, and they seized it. They went on a record-breaking hiring spree, bringing in more than 350,000 seasonal workers nationwide to meet the country's new demands in the face of the pandemic.

For us workers, it was a different story. At JFK8, and elsewhere, we were treated as disposable. We still had to report to work every day or risk losing our jobs. We watched people coming in visibly sick. Keep in mind, Amazon didn't have sick days. There was only unpaid time off for most of us, which you could be fired for using, even during a pandemic. The whole situation created a lot of fear, confusion, and anger.

Danielle Hayden is a union member and member of our executive board who also came to JFK8 when the building first opened, like me. She has cerebral palsy and often advocates for workers with disabilities. When the pandemic hit, she was frustrated like the rest of us because Amazon didn't provide any kind of sanitizers, masks, or gloves, or enforce social distancing. We now know of at least three workers who were on the job and later died from Covid, but Amazon didn't make any of that public at the time. Danielle was very vocal about these problems. Right from the start, she was bringing her own PPE to work with her.

Meanwhile, the company told us nothing. We didn't even know how many people inside the building had already tested positive or died. On March 24, Chris confronted a supervisor who was walking around sluggishly, with bloodshot eyes, wearing a mask. She admitted that she had tested positive for Covid. But at that point she'd already worked several ten-hour days in a row, alongside hundreds of people. Why wasn't she home? This was it for us.

Chris immediately came downstairs and got me. He was like, "Yo. I just had a meeting with the managers and PAs and they told us that someone tested positive for Covid and that we shouldn't tell anyone."

I said, "What?! Are you serious?! We need to get out of here." And that's exactly what we did. We left around noon that day. The next day, March 25, we stood at the entrance of the building informing workers that they were trying to hide that someone had tested positive for Covid. After that, we went straight to the break room to let people know what was going on. We started yelling at the top of our lungs that the building needed to be closed and sanitized. We came back every day, for three days, with this message. We'd already seen in the news that an Amazon warehouse in Kentucky was closed by the governor, and we had no doubt that JFK8 needed to do the same thing.

By Saturday, March 28, Chris and I were feeling defeated and angry that management wouldn't close the building. As we sat in the break room, a senior leader walked up to Chris and told him he needed to leave because he had allegedly been in contact with someone who had tested positive. He didn't say anything about me having to leave. Afterward, we sat in the parking lot for a minute. Chris looked at me and said, "We're going to have to do a walkout." I said, "Yes, let's do it." We went to Chris's house and called the Department of Labor and OSHA to report conditions in the building. We also started a group chat and contacted some reporters to let them know we were planning to walk out on March 30.

Covid was, for all of us, our tipping point.

It's what led Chris and me to plan our now famous walkout on March 30, 2020. Looking back, I wonder what would have happened if Amazon had put in place basic safety measures. We weren't asking for much, just that they close the building for a fourteen-day period to sanitize it and implement the use of PPE. If they had at least addressed some of our concerns, we might not even have a union today. Their biggest mistake was that they did nothing.

The Congress of Essential Workers (TCOEW)

During the pandemic, Amazon workers were categorized as "essential workers" along with teachers, bus drivers, health care workers, and others who continued to show up to their jobs. This meant that we had to go to work even if the company knowingly put us in danger. Our frustrations were building, and we had a lot of complicated emotions. We felt angry with the company for not doing the right thing to keep the workers safe, but there was also the fear of retaliation if we took the next step of organizing a walkout. Still, we were determined to get the building shut down so that it could be cleaned. We wanted to show workers that there was power in speaking their minds and that our voices as a collective mattered.

On March 28, the day Amazon put Chris on a "quarantine leave," he and I sat in my car trying to figure out what to do. We decided we were out of options, and we began to plan a walkout for March 30. On our way home, we called Gerald and Jordan so they could start spreading the word. I created an Instagram group chat and added everyone I knew at Amazon so they could mobilize workers inside as well.

By the time March 30 rolled around, about fifty of us were prepared to walk out. Chris and I both reached out to multiple news outlets. We knew we were going to make history but weren't quite sure what that would look like yet. At the time, the walkout was supposed to be a single action. We had no intention of becoming a union. Not yet, at least. As we approached the building that morning, the first thing we saw was a row of media vans and a helicopter hovering above.

Amazon's secret was out.

That was when Amazon made another one of its biggest blunders: they fired Chris. Not only did they fire him, but even worse, the company's chief counsel, David Zapolsky, wrote an internal memo that he sent out to a company LISTSERV of about one thousand people. It contained notes from a daily meeting that Bezos attended, where Zapolsky described Chris as "not smart or articulate." He put his foot in his mouth *big*-time. Zapolsky went on to say that focusing on Chris would be a good PR strategy because it would make him "the face of the entire organizing/labor movement" and discredit our budding campaign.

In his notes, Zapolsky made it clear that others who'd attended the meeting agreed with this strategy. He's still Chief of Global Affairs and Legal Officer today. That tells you all you need to know right there about how companies like Amazon work. They made a huge wrong turn that day. Chris already *was* the face of the movement, but what Zapolsky and Bezos didn't realize was that his brash, outspoken leadership style was exactly what workers were drawn to. Maybe the suits at Amazon didn't understand it, but Chris's authenticity resonated with workers.

We turned up the volume on what we were doing.

In April, we organized another walkout to let people know we weren't stopping. This time, Gerald Bryson was suspended and later fired. Amazon also gave me a final write-up for violating social distancing, which was laughable. They didn't have any social distancing! That was the problem, and the whole reason we walked out. But they tried to turn it around and use that against me when I was the one advocating for the safety of workers. One day shortly afterward, Chris and I were at his apartment when we finally decided to take the next big step. Workers from other companies like Target and Starbucks had been contacting us in support and solidarity since we began our actions. Now we made plans to form what we called the Congress of Essential Workers, an informal collective of allies who came together to fight for better working conditions and higher wages.

Obviously, the company appeared to be retaliating against us. But in my case, they failed because I had researched my rights. I knew that you weren't supposed to get a "final write-up" out of nowhere. Company policy was that you would first get a warning. After that, you would normally get something called "documented coaching." There was a first write-up, a second write-up, and only after all of that happened would you get a final write-up.

Gerald and I both hired a lawyer named Frank Kearl. Make the Road New York, a nonprofit organization that fights for immigrants and working-class people to achieve justice in their communities, reached out to us after the March 30, 2020, walkout at JFK8. Frank was one of their attorneys, and he wanted to work with us. Gerald filed an Unfair Labor Practice (ULP) case against Amazon with the National Labor Relations Board (NLRB) for wrongful termination. In my case, Frank and I decided that our best move would be to file a public nuisance case because this wasn't about me, individually. It was about what we could do, legally, to help push the entire movement forward. We felt like the public nuisance case was our strongest move. Amazon didn't see that one coming at all. I don't think they expected us to know how to file lawsuits.

Our friend Jordan Flowers, the fourth cofounder of TCOEW, was already out of the building when the pandemic hit. Jordan came to work at JFK8 in 2018, the day the building opened, at the age of eighteen. He was the baby among us. He worked in Robotics, where he kept watch over three hundred robots that brought pods to the Pick stations.

One of the reasons Jordan wanted to work at Amazon was for the health care benefits. At age twelve, he'd been diagnosed with lupus. His goal was to make enough money to be able to go back to school at the College of Staten Island, where he was studying to become a physical therapist.

Jordan also had high blood pressure, and previously in 2019, he had to be hospitalized for a night. He was scheduled to work the next day but his doctor said he needed to stay out for three days. Jordan gave his medical absence letter to HR, but what happened next made no sense. His leave was denied, and eventually Amazon started deducting from his unpaid time, which ended up resulting in an unfair termination. He fought it and ended up being hired back that same year.

But not long after, Jordan suffered a knee injury and had to go out again. His job in Robotics required a lot of walking and he wasn't moving as fast as he had been before. He was finally about to come back to work when Covid hit in early 2020. Being immunocompromised and with no PPE to use, there was no way he was going to come back into the building. Jordan always says the same thing about that choice: "I'm my mom's only child. I wasn't going to lose my life for a company that doesn't care about me."

Throughout the pandemic, our group continued fighting, and we became a movement. TCOEW held rallies and visited other Amazon facilities so that we could become more educated about what was going on company-wide. We set up a GoFundMe account to help pay for our travel. I know that Chris paid some out of his own pocket, too.

We did a Google search to find out where Bezos had his mansions and penthouses and protested in front of as many as we could. We went to his $80 million triplex penthouse on East Twenty-Sixth Street and Fifth Avenue in Manhattan, where he'd basically combined three apartments for a total of seventeen thousand square feet and twelve bedrooms. Our New York Labor Day rally brought in around three thousand supporters from all over the country. We even shut down Times Square.

We also hit Bezos's $23 million mansion in Washington, DC, and his $24 million Beverly Hills mansion with seven bedrooms and a six-car garage. (I heard he later bought the home next door, too, for another $12 million.) Unfortunately, we couldn't get to them all. We missed his $90 million spread on Indian Creek Island in Miami. Even if we'd tried, I doubt we would have gotten near that one. Indian Creek Island is known as "Billionaire Bunker" and has its own private police force and around-the-clock armed boat patrols. Today, Bezos owns at least three homes there, valued at around $234 million. We also missed his $78 million fourteen-acre compound in Maui, Hawaii, and his four-hundred-thousand-acre ranch near Van Horn, Texas, not to mention other residences in California, New York, and Seattle.

We did get to Amazon headquarters in Seattle, though, where we were joined by around a dozen local activists. Security forces at the building immediately told us we couldn't be there, but we went ahead and gave our speeches on the front steps anyway, just before marching through the streets of downtown Seattle.

We were fired up, and still are. And instead of letting our anger eat us up inside, we used it to ignite and fuel an entirely new labor movement. We directed it outward, to target what we believed was the greed and inhumanity of Amazon. The pandemic was our atomic moment. In fact, it was the atomic moment for a lot of workers in industries throughout America. We now know this is true because ever since Covid, union support has increased and is now at 71 percent, according to Gallup polls, higher than it has been since 1965.

Using Your Anger for Change

I'm a ten-year veteran at Amazon now. After my first three years, I stopped getting raises, except for the basic cost of living and inflation increases. Today, I'm maxed out at $24.25 an hour. Over the past decade, a sense of righteous anger has taught me some important lessons, especially about myself.

Some workers can become intimidated by management, but for whatever reason, that has never been the case for me. I've learned that I'm not afraid to be vocal. Anytime I've heard about a fellow worker being mistreated, I've always gone immediately to the main office where all the managers are—the senior operations managers and the general manager—and approached them directly about it.

At first, I vented my frustrations directly through my anger, getting into heated back-and-forth discussions with managers, to the point that they tried to label me as an "angry Black guy." Eventually, I saw that it wasn't working. I've learned that yelling at the top of your lungs isn't a good look for anyone. So I shifted that energy, using my anger to help other people.

You can use your anger in many ways to help and inspire others. You can speak out at a captive audience meeting or organize a march. For example, when a worker is angry about constantly being sent to another department, I first try to calm them down. Then I educate them about how the company is trying to save money by making them perform multiple duties instead of hiring another worker. This is the moment when they begin to understand the importance of getting a contract and being able to negotiate collectively for a work jurisdiction clause or job classification clause, which protect workers from being reassigned outside their regular department without consent, bargaining, or extra pay. Instead of being angry about it, this worker may now start to feel more empowered and be able to inspire others to fight for change as well. Anger can be a powerful force for change if you use it in the correct way.

No one can stop an atomic moment from coming. As organizers, we need to find the courage to use those strong emotions to propel us forward to the next step, to dive in and use our energy. After an atomic moment, organizers need to let that anger fuel action. First, get educated. Learn about your rights. Learn about the history of unions. Learn what you can and cannot change at your workplace. Educate yourself. Then start the work of educating others.

What Is a Union?

Let's take a step back. The simple definition of a "union" is "a group of workers collectively advocating for their rights." A union provides strength through numbers, which allows workers to negotiate for things like higher wages, better benefits, safety measures, and job security. The goal of a union is not to tear down a workplace but to make it fairer for workers.

Most of us instinctively understand this. In a September 2024 Gallup poll, about 77 percent of Americans thought labor unions "mostly help" workers. At the same time, 61 percent thought unions "mostly help" the U.S. economy as well. When asked if major corporations have "too much power," 67 percent agreed.

Overseas, and especially in Europe, unions are often seen even more favorably than they are here in the U.S. Amazon facilities in Italy and Germany have unions. All those brothers and sisters are organized, but they'll never tell you that at JFK8. They'll never tell you about how, in Quebec, Canada, Amazon workers came so close to unionizing that, rather than dealing with them fairly, Amazon decided in 2025 to shut the whole operation down, closing all its warehouses there, and laying off seventeen hundred employees.

While we may instinctively favor unions, the sad fact is that most Americans don't know much about their important role in this country. We don't realize that so many of the protections we take for granted came out of organized labor. Without unions there would be no sick leave, no weekends, no vacation time, no child labor protection laws, and no overtime pay. Before we started the ALU, I didn't know any of this, either. I assumed these were things that we just always had. Learning the true history was mind-blowing to me.

When we first decided to create the Congress of Essential Workers in 2020, Chris, Gerald, Jordan, and I all did our own research into labor union history. Some of us had family members who had been in unions. Chris's mom, then an administrative assistant at Mount Sinai Beth Israel in New York City, had been a member of the 1199SEIU United Healthcare Workers East years earlier. Jordan's mother and grandmother were both nurses with the 1199, and Jordan has clear memories of the union paying for his summer camp and helping him go to the YMCA. The union even provided food for his family when times were rough.

In my own family, my uncle Andre had been with the International Longshoremen's Association (ILA). He worked extremely long days, averaging 110 hours a week, but I know he was happy with the benefits he got through the union: excellent pay, health coverage (medical, dental, and vision), and his 401(k) retirement account.

Our cofounder Gerald Bryson had personally been in several different unions before coming to Amazon, including DC 37, New York City's largest public-employee union, and the 1199SEIU, back when he worked in janitorial services at Sea View Hospital on Staten Island. He knew firsthand some of the benefits unions provided, and was eager to share with us.

Learning from History

I've always admired Dr. Martin Luther King Jr. and his Poor People's Campaign. When I started researching labor history, I learned more about the day he was assassinated, April 4, 1968. Dr. King was in Memphis, Tennessee, that day to support thirteen hundred striking sanitation workers who had walked off the job after two employees were crushed to death by a garbage truck compactor. The workers stayed on strike for sixty-four days, demanding higher wages and an end to the city's racist and inhumane treatment. They famously held up placards that said, "I am a man." Which is not that much different, if you think about it, from the Amazon signs many workers now hold saying, "I am not a robot."

But we can go back even further to see how important unions have been in America, especially for Black people. In 1925, A. Philip Randolph organized the Brotherhood of Sleeping Car Porters. Later, he served as a vice president of the American Federation of Labor and Congress of Industrial Organizations (AFL-CIO), the largest federation of unions in the country, with more than sixty national and international member organizations. Bayard Rustin, the mastermind behind the 1963 March on Washington, was also on the executive council of the AFL-CIO. Mary McLeod Bethune, who started a school for Black girls in Florida, was elected the first woman president of the National Association of Teachers in Colored Schools in the 1920s. This was a union that would later merge with the National Education Association. The list of Black civil rights leaders who were also involved with unions goes on and on.

Black people in America have always recognized the need for solidarity among workers of all backgrounds. What we were doing with TCOEW and the ALU wasn't new. Instead, we were just adding a fresh take on a long tradition of Black activism and resistance.

In the beginning stages of our movement, I started searching the internet to learn more about the goals and methods of other unions. I looked at the International Brotherhood of Teamsters (IBT), America's largest union, founded in 1903; the SEIU; the United Food and Commercial Workers International Union (UFCW); and the Retail, Wholesale and Department Store Union (RWDSU), for example. I remember the four of us founders also talked about the International Brotherhood of Electrical Workers in Chicago (IBEW) because, although they were affiliated with the AFL-CIO, their union was founded on the idea of local autonomy, something we knew we had to have.

Education and reflection have always been a core part of the ALU. That's why our first website featured Dr. King's teachings on labor. It's also why we gave out free books at our rallies. We didn't have a formal list of titles; our goal was to share knowledge and inspiration wherever we found it. I remember we had a shared copy of the bestseller *The 48 Laws of Power* by Robert Greene that we passed around, along with *Letters to a Young Brother: Manifest Your Destiny* by the actor and activist Hill Harper. Another favorite of ours was *The Art of War*, written by the Chinese military strategist and philosopher Sun Tzu around the fifth century BC.

Successful organizers must be informed. There's no way around it. As activist Jane McAlevey said, there are no shortcuts to organizing. When we started preparing our campaign, we knew we needed to research, study, and learn as much as we could. I truly believe that one of the reasons we won our election was that Amazon underestimated us. They had no idea how prepared we were, in our hearts and in our minds.

Eight Signs That You Might Need a Union

How do you know if you need a union at your job? How can you be sure it's the right decision? The only way you're going to know the answer to these questions is by studying your specific work environment. Every workplace is different. You might have five employees or five thousand. Start by learning the ins and outs of your employer. Go to the company's website and look up their policies. Read the employee handbook. See what you're allowed to do and what you're not allowed to do. You need to intimately understand the company's practices. And only then can you see if they're living up to their stated goals and values. To be a successful organizer, you absolutely cannot skip this step.

Here is a list of some signs that you might need a union:

1. Unsafe or inhumane working conditions
2. Lack of communication between management and workers
3. Mandatory overtime/holiday shifts
4. Lack of sick days
5. Lack of benefits
6. High turnover rate
7. Favoritism and discrimination
8. Lack of promotions and raises

You'll have to judge what's acceptable to you and your coworkers, and what isn't. In our case at JFK8, all eight of these issues were problems. So, for us, the need to start a union was obvious.

The first sign is so pervasive and so important that it deserves special attention because so many American workplaces have **unsafe or inhumane conditions**. Oftentimes, this issue is where workers draw the line. Who wants to go to clock in somewhere wondering if they'll make it back home in one piece? Who wants to feel dehumanized just because they need to use the bathroom? Who wants to go to a job that chips away at their dignity every day? Unsafe or inhumane conditions may look different depending on where you work; your situation may not be as extreme as ours, but by showing you some of the problems we faced at Amazon, hopefully I can help you make your own decision on taking action.

At Amazon, unsafe and inhumane conditions are well-known and well-documented all around the world. Just look at how they hire and fire people. When you apply to work at an Amazon warehouse, you don't need to submit any kind of résumé. There's no job interview. It really is that they're hiring as fast as they can to chew people up and spit them back out. If you get injured, they move on to the next one. That's why some Amazon campaigns have adopted the slogan "I am not a robot." The management culture of Amazon makes it clear that turnover is high by design. If you talk to workers there, they'll mention simple indignities. Like the fact that you're not even given a step stool to sit on for an eleven- or twelve-hour shift. You can take your two thirty-minute breaks, but other than that, expect to be on your feet the whole time, in constant motion, reacting to robot pods that come to you at a lightning-fast pace.

Another indignity is Amazon's penalty policy for "time off task" (TOT), which even the State of New York has recognized as dehumanizing and illegal. It works like this: If you step away from your station, the computer checks the last item scanned before you left, and the first item scanned when you return. This way, it automatically generates a notification to management showing how long you were away. Maybe you weren't feeling well and went to the bathroom. Or maybe you went to the vending machine to get a bottle of water. Or you got a call from your kid's school and stepped away to take it. It doesn't really matter what your reason is. Six minutes off task? You can easily get written up and penalized for the time you were gone.

Amazon knows that their quotas are brutal. They know that workers are stressed out by being written up and penalized for TOT. There are workers who even skip breaks and meals just to be sure they reach their quotas. Not only are penalties harsh, but they're also enforced randomly. If you have TOT, a manager is supposed to talk to you about it. But instead, they often just let it become an automatic write-up. Why? Because the more write-ups you have, the higher the turnover rate, and managers with too few write-ups can get a write-up themselves.

In 2023, New York State passed the Warehouse Worker Protection Act to create more transparency about these practices. But so far, it seems that Amazon has mostly ignored the new law. For example, the law states that a written explanation must be provided for every write-up. Workers should also be entitled to see their production numbers and to be able to compare them with those of other associates doing the same job. As far as I can see, that's not happening at JFK8. Instead, management will tell someone only that they're in the "bottom 3 percent" or something like that, with no data to compare that figure to.

Safety issues are also well-known at Amazon, from minor injuries to severe. In July 2022, a worker named Rafael Reynaldo Mota Frias, forty-two, had a heart attack at Amazon's EWR9 in New Jersey and died. He was working during Prime Day rush when temperatures were in the nineties. Amazon denied wrongdoing, and an OSHA investigation later found that his death was due to a preexisting medical condition. Still, the next month Amazon installed a new air-conditioning system and additional fans in the facility, which was interesting timing to say the least.

At JFK8, a worker named Terica Clark got involved with the ALU in part because she experienced safety problems. In August 2021, Terica was injured while trying to get a pod out of a box. She used the correct form and grip, but the box slid and jammed her thumb against the metal. When she went to AMCARE, Amazon's on-site first-aid clinic, she said no one there even bothered to explain her right to time off. The next day, she clocked back in as usual with her hand wrapped. It wasn't until she went to human resources on a different issue, and they were made aware of her injury, that she was given workers' compensation papers and sent home. I remember she told me, "I'm so grateful for that HR rep who noticed, because if it wasn't for her, I'd still be clocking in like a dummy."

At Amazon, these kinds of injuries happen every single day, and just like in Terica's case, they're often overlooked. Terica also had surgery on both hands for bilateral carpal tunnel syndrome. In the end, Amazon ended up firing her. She filed a ULP complaint with the NLRB and became a big supporter of the ALU. She later helped us pass out flyers, attended meetings, and stood up to union busters. What every organizer needs to understand is that workers like Terica, and anyone else, have a right, by law, to talk to other workers about safety issues and to help others understand their rights. It's powerful to learn about stories like hers and to know that there are things we can all do to protect ourselves. Again, your situation might not look like ours, or be as extreme. But we all know when something is unsafe or inhumane—and more likely than not, you're not alone in thinking it.

The second sign that you might need a union is **a lack of communication between management and workers**. Many companies like to make the argument that the union is a "third party," meaning a group of people or a person that isn't directly involved at the workplace. Union busters use this terminology to persuade workers that the company has the workers' best interest at heart and that organizers are simply "outsiders." They'll say that it's better to work with the company "directly." That's their spin. But what if the voices of workers are being ignored? What if workers are pointing out problems and nothing is being done? How is that a "direct" relationship?

At Amazon, we have something called the Voice of Associates (VOA) board, which is a platform for workers to flag issues or express their dissatisfaction. At JFK8, you can see this signage posted on the first and third floors of the facility, and we also have it on our phones, on the A to Z app that we use to access employee information. If you post a complaint there it shows your face, your login, and your comment. Supposedly, you can post anonymously, but most people I know don't believe that their posts are anonymous. We all know that there's no such thing as confidentiality when it comes to Amazon. The company can easily track posts and find out who they're from.

Once you post on the VOA board, there will usually be a reply from a senior manager. But here's the problem with this so-called direct communication. I won't say the responses are exactly computer generated, but they can feel that way. They're vague and noncommittal. What's worse is that most managers use a standard line, offering to "meet you in person to discuss the matter" as a solution.

But the VOA board is supposedly there exactly for that reason: to get direct answers and solutions in a prompt, stress-free way, without having to meet in person. I know from experience that most workers aren't comfortable talking to HR, or any supervisor with a vest for that matter, except maybe their direct manager. Meeting with a manager in person is just another opportunity to intimidate somebody. I believe they know this and are well aware that Amazon's system of "open communication" doesn't do what it's supposed to do.

In February 2025, there were several posts from workers who were angry about the company's frequent job rotations. They were tired of being bounced to different departments "like Ping-Pong." A worker named Javine wrote in all caps, "STOP SENDING ME TO PICK EVERYDAY AT 12:15 AM." He said the company was pulling the same people to go to this one shift every day, and he wanted to know why. The answer came from Jack, a senior operations manager, who said he was "sorry to hear about this experience." He then said that an operations manager named Adam would follow up in person on Javine's next scheduled shift "in order to provide support."

That kind of response is, in my view, nothing but intimidation. I know because management tried to use my VOA posts against me all the time. After I posted, two or three days later, someone from HR would come up to me on the floor. Sometimes even a group of them would show up to talk to me. How is that supposed to make workers feel? Now everyone is staring at you, thinking you must be in some kind of trouble. Fortunately, their little scare tactics didn't work with me. I faced whoever came to talk to me with the same energy I had when I first posted on the VOA board.

Does your manager or supervisor bully and intimidate you? Are you able to voice legitimate concerns about safety and conditions on the job? Are you being moved to different departments or being asked to take on new duties without your consent? Are the responses to your concerns appropriate? These are all questions you might want to ask yourself when considering whether you need a union.

Moving on to number three on our list, all I can say is, if you're working somewhere where **overtime and/or working over holidays is mandatory**, that's automatically a problem. Numbers four and five are related to number three, given that **a lack of sick days and/or benefits** often makes work mandatory. Every peak season at Amazon, from November 23 to December 24, workers are expected to increase from a ten-hour shift to an eleven- or twelve-hour shift. They might also add an extra day of work to your schedule. So you could end up with five straight days of eleven-hour shifts. Also, once the schedule is posted, it's mandatory. There's nothing you can do to change it.

If you were hoping to travel or to spend the holidays with family, that's pretty much impossible, too. The company only gives out fifty-six hours of personal time for the entire year, which includes sick days. And you can only accumulate these hours between January and May. This means that by the time peak season starts, most people have already run out of those five days, making working during this season essentially mandatory.

As I mentioned before, Jordan Flowers, one of our cofounders, has systemic lupus. If he's sick with anything, even something as simple as a cold, he's most likely going to be out for much longer than other people. For him, a cold can take him down for even as long as two weeks.

But after those fifty-six hours are gone, your only option around the holidays is to ask for a leave of absence without pay, which usually, in my experience, won't be given anyway. Not during peak season.

I met my good friend Ashley Nelson because she had an issue with HR after having a wisdom tooth pulled. She ended up with a serious infection and needed emergency surgery. Her whole face was swollen, and she stayed in the hospital for more than a week. What's amazing is that during that whole time, Amazon was calling her, even while she was still in the hospital, and saying she needed to work.

She had only been home recovering for three days when Amazon said she needed to come in or lose her job. Ashley had two kids at the time (now three). She couldn't afford to lose her job, so she went to work. I can't imagine what that must have been like. Her wound was still open, with pus and blood leaking out from beneath the gauze. She was on all kinds of different medications and disoriented.

But she still made the almost three-hour commute from her home in Upper Manhattan to Staten Island. When she got to the building, they told her she was going to be put in Stow, a position in which the machine comes right up to you. You can't do that kind of dangerous work in a state like hers. To add even more insult to injury, her manager insisted that she *clock out* to take her medications. He said she couldn't do that on Amazon's time.

I took up her case on behalf of the ALU, going back and forth with HR and Disability and Leave Services for several weeks until, finally, we were able to resolve the issue, owing to a specific strategy. To this day, Amazon refuses to recognize the ALU. Sometimes people ask me how I'm able to advocate for workers on the inside if we have no bargaining power. My answer is this: I come prepared with arguments that are in the company's best interest.

In Ashley's case, I explained to management that it was detrimental *to them* to have her working at a station while she was still bleeding, especially after we'd just fought off Covid. That's not safe for anyone. "You can't preach that you care about families, health, and safety when you're doing things like this," I said, and it worked. This is a clear example of when and why union representatives are needed. When workers' voices are not being heard, we bring a seriousness and intention to the conversation that force companies to pay attention.

Have you been disciplined, or fired unfairly, for being ill or for having an emergency? Does your company listen to your concerns regarding hours and scheduling, taking into consideration medical, childcare, and family needs? If you answered yes to this first question, and/or answered no to the second, then you may need a union to help advocate for your basic rights.

Ever since that fight, Ashley has become an important member of our team. She's now on our executive board and advocates for other workers, just like I do. She grew up in the same neighborhood where the number 40 bus line passes, carrying Amazon workers into JFK8 every single day. She understands what they go through because she went through it herself.

We've already discussed the last three signs you might need a union, numbers six, seven, and eight. But as a reminder, here are some more questions to ask yourself: Does your company hire and fire indiscriminately, using a **high turnover rate** to especially avoid paying for health care and benefits and to increase profits? Is there **favoritism and discrimination**? Are there opportunities to move up in the company and to **earn promotions and raises**? Or are workers stuck, trapped in low-paying, entry-level positions despite hard work and seniority?

Deciding whether your workplace needs a union is something every organizer needs to consider on their own. It's not going to look the same for everyone. But what is undeniable from our perspective is that having someone stand beside you in solidarity on any of these eight problems—or any other problem that impacts us as both humans and workers—could only be a benefit. That's why we organize.

Everyone Matters, Leave No One Behind

Here are two core concepts at the heart of the Amazon Labor Union: Everyone matters. Leave no one behind.

I once went to battle with HR for a worker named Brittany Garcia. She was a single mom who commuted to JFK8 from the Bronx on public transportation. She asked for a schedule change, which HR approved but then never gave to her. After that, she was suddenly terminated. Brittany, who was a full-time worker, filed a ULP with the NLRB as well as an ethics claim with Amazon. We fought hard for her, and she eventually got her job back. But that wasn't the end of the story.

Brittany has a sister named Sarah who was a seasonal worker at Amazon. She was a university student who needed accommodation in her schedule to take classes. Instead, immediately after Brittany filed her case, they put Sarah on a leave of absence. In my opinion, this was a clear act of retaliation. So we fought for Sarah, too.

Everyone matters. Leave no one behind.

After our union was certified, the Staten Island building stopped hiring full-time, or blue badge, workers. Today, they only hire the white badge seasonal workers, most of whom are there year-round, despite the misleading title. That says a lot. In my view it tells us that the company's strategy is to weed us full-time workers out. There are advantages to this for Amazon. Seasonal workers are cheaper than full-time workers and they typically don't receive benefits. I've known some seasonal workers who are homeless or living in a trailer home. What they earn is not enough to survive on.

After the union was voted in, however, that changed somewhat.

As of October 2024, Amazon started giving flex, temp, and part-time workers health benefits, which was long overdue. That tells me that the company felt the pressure of our collective action. This was their way of trying to save face.

Day shift, night shift, temp, flex, seasonal—it doesn't matter where you are in the chain or where you work. We're all workers. Everyone matters. Leave no one behind.

2.

Getting Started

Three Things You Need to Know

Before starting your organizing campaign there are three pieces of information you need to know. These are: **basic federal labor law**, **the laws within your state**, and **the specific policies inside your company**.

I learned so much from the website of the National Labor Relations Board (https://www.nlrb.gov/) at the start of our campaign. Honestly, it was my main source of information for understanding more about federal labor law and its history in this country. For example, I discovered that when unions were at their height in this country during the 1930s, 27 percent of U.S. workers were union members! That is a lot of people. Imagine if today one out of every three or four people you knew belonged to a union? Unions would be so common that they'd be seen as part of ordinary, everyday life.

The NLRB was established with the Wagner Act of 1935 with the simple goal of ensuring that workers had the right to come together in collective action. It's a small, independent federal agency that continues to protect this right at the national level. I learned incredible things about organizing by studying some of this history. For one thing, I learned that you can't legally be fired for organizing a walkout. And you can't legally be fired for speaking up about workplace safety issues. Something else I learned was that company managers can't remove union literature, just like workers can't remove anti-union literature, either. It's imperative you understand federal labor law before going forward.

As we prepared, we were meticulous in our research, making sure we followed all the laws to a T. Unfortunately, as I understand the law, I can't say the same for Amazon. Even though I believe they knew they were in violation of federal law, they repeatedly threw away our literature and ripped down our signs. This isn't unusual; some companies violate labor law every day. That's a bigger structural problem that I'll come back to later in the book. For now, let's just say that workers do have **federally protected rights** on the job, and to be successful, you need to know exactly what they are.

The U.S. Department of Labor (https://www.dol.gov/) is another helpful resource that has a wealth of information. Under "Topics" you can learn about everything from the rights of new mothers, to equal employment and anti-discrimination laws, to protections for whistleblowers. This is a massive department with dozens of agencies that are there to assist workers, such as the Occupational Safety and Health Administration (OSHA), which does inspections of job sites, for example, and the Office of Workers' Compensation Programs (OWCP), which can provide helpful information after an accident or injury.

It also publishes information about the federal minimum wage, which is currently just $7.25 if you can believe it—a number that hasn't gone up since 2009. There are twenty states that still, even today, keep to this minimum wage. Other states have better protection for workers. We're fortunate that in New York we have a higher minimum wage than most places, either $16.50 or $15.50 depending on your county. But we need it, given the extremely high cost of living here. Washington State has a higher minimum wage than us, at $16.66 per hour, as does Washington, DC, at $17.50. It's a helpful guide for determining if your company is above or below average for your state, and whether you might need to fight for a wage that keeps up with the cost of living in your area.

Once you've got the basics of federal labor law down—your rights as a worker, what the employer is allowed to do, and everything in between—you need to understand **the laws in your state**. Some states are more friendly to unions than others. In so-called right-to-work states, for example, which are most states in the country, unions can't require workers to contribute union fees even if they benefit from bargaining agreements and contracts.

In New York, we have more protection than in many states. In 2023, the ALU and other supporters of workers' rights celebrated a major win here with the passage of the Warehouse Worker Protection Act. This was specifically designed to rein in the abuses of Amazon and to protect workers from inhumane conditions and unfair terminations. The act states that if companies like Amazon want workers to function at a high speed and to make quotas, they need to be transparent and tell workers exactly what that speed is. Until the Protection Act was put in place, that particular information wasn't available to us. In my experience, workers were being fired for not making a quota when they didn't even know what that quota was!

The law also says we have a right to see our "personal work speed data" and to be able to compare that to data for similar employees. It also protects employees from retaliation if they ask for this information or file a related complaint. Finally, the law says that quotas can't be so unreasonable that they interfere with "lawful meal or rest periods or use of bathroom facilities"—which is something Amazon workers have been saying for a long time. Amazon is required to offer a thirty-minute lunch break, but depending on where your station is, it might take ten minutes to get to and from a break room. So how could that add up to a thirty-minute rest period? Now New York's law stipulates that workers must be given "reasonable travel time" to and from the bathroom. These are all victories won by our organizing efforts.

Right now, there are more than a dozen states that have introduced legislation similar to the Warehouse Worker Protection Act. Organizers should know if their state is one of them and work to support these legislative and policy efforts. More broadly, organizers need to keep track of state laws in case they either support or hinder unions.

In addition to federal and state law, the third kind of information organizers need to understand are the **specific**

policies of their own companies. You'll need to be able to identify flaws in these policies and where your company is falling short. Amazon loves to say that they provide great benefits, but these benefits aren't always as advertised. For example, the company says they offer college tuition. That actually refers to something they call "Career Choice." It's not exactly college tuition that you can use anywhere. Instead, Career Choice is a program where Amazon will pay for workers to learn a specific trade, like transportation or coding and billing. Basically, the funding is limited to Amazon industries and positions.

Their supposed paid family leave has a lot of flaws, too. Why is it that when workers try to go on family leave, they always have trouble with HR and management? In so many cases that I've seen, Amazon is not giving employees the amount of pay that they're supposed to receive when on family leave. Or they're "accidentally" terminating workers who were supposed to be on leaves. There have always been problems with this particular benefit at JFK8. I know my friend Ashley Nelson had a lot of issues with her maternity leave, and she knows plenty of women in the building who can tell the same story.

It's important to be able to identify the gap between policy and reality in your company's advertised benefits. I'm fortunate to have health care coverage as a full-time blue badge worker. But the copay is seventy-five dollars. That's a lot for most workers. Coworkers I know would have to be very sick to go to a doctor, knowing they'll need to pay seventy-five dollars every single time. If you plan to organize your workplace, you'll need to not only be able to articulate the flaws behind these policies but also eventually explain what better options might look like.

Companies with unions have better benefits and higher wages than those without unions. We know this for a fact. But as an organizer you'll need to break this down to help other workers understand why better options are not being delivered to them, even though the company says they are. Without a detailed understanding of the company, its benefits, and workers' rights, you won't be able to convince people to sign authorization cards.

This may all be starting to feel overwhelming. You're working a job and now suddenly I'm saying you need to go home and study state and federal law in your spare time? I know that can feel like a lot, which is exactly why every organizer and every team needs to get **a labor lawyer** as soon as possible.

Finding a Labor Lawyer

Labor law is its own complex area of specialization. It's not something most people understand. After studying up, we realized there were still significant gaps in our knowledge. So we put out a call for legal help on Twitter very early on, before we even started our campaign. It basically said, "Hey, we're looking for a labor lawyer!" Looking back, this was such an important step. You want to get someone on board right from the start so that the company might think twice before retaliating against you.

After that post, we got a DM from a labor lawyer in New York named Seth Goldstein. Seth had been doing this work for a very long time, helping workers in the tech industry and at companies like Trader Joe's. We were lucky that Seth more or less fell into our lap. He believed in us and was passionate about helping our cause. For about a year and a half, he worked with us pro bono. But even if you're fortunate enough to find a good pro bono lawyer, there are still massive costs involved. A transcript from an NLRB hearing can cost as much as thirty thousand dollars! The system is set up so that a worker needs money just to be able to participate in the process.

Seth would guide us every step of the way, warning us, "Don't do this" or "Don't do that." He knew every angle of labor law. I liked how he would just bust out and start talking about *The Harbor*, one of the first socialist books in America, published in 1915, as part of a conversation. We all felt like it was fate that he came along when he did.

Seth was also able to educate us about what laws he believed Amazon was breaking, which was crucial information. The first day of our **union drive** was April 20, 2021. This is the moment when we officially began trying to gain support from employees to create a union. Immediately, Amazon tried to kick us off the property, despite us being at a bus stop. That was their first attempt at busting our union.

We set up our music with a speaker connected to a generator and they tried to call the fire department on us, saying we needed a permit. But the fire department came and said that actually we did not need one. We'd done our research ahead of time and we knew that the bus stop was on city grounds. We were within our rights, and we knew that Amazon wasn't going to be able to get rid of us there, and they never did. But that doesn't mean they didn't keep trying.

The company violated our right to unionize so many times and in so many ways. In the JFK8 parking lot, we were legally allowed to campaign by passing out union literature and getting authorization cards signed, but Amazon tried to kick us out of there, too, which was in violation of federal law. And this wasn't just happening at JFK8. Other Amazon workers in Ohio and Illinois were also being told by security that they couldn't be there supporting unionizing, either.

No matter how early you are in the process of organizing, trust me, you need a lawyer. We were up against a multitrillion-dollar company with something like six lawyers fighting for them full-time. They're each making something crazy, like $1,500 an hour, just to file objections to everything we do. Their plan is simple: to wear the union down and run out the clock. They know that with Amazon's high turnover rate, which is currently 150 percent, most of the union's core leaders will eventually leave or be fired, and if they drag out their objections long enough, we'll have to start our campaign all over again.

Look at the Smithfield hog processing plant in Tar Heel, North Carolina, a rural, impoverished area in a **right-to-work state**. The NLRB ruled that the company was guilty of unfair labor practices during two union elections, in 1994 and 1997, but Smithfield lawyers successfully delayed and appealed. In 2008, after sixteen years of fighting, workers there finally did what most people never imagined they would be able to do: they voted yes to the union.

Without a labor lawyer, there's no way we would've gotten off the ground. Make sure you find yours.

Authorization Cards: What They Are and Why They're Important

Authorization cards are simple. They're three-by-five index cards with your full name and signature, stating that you want to be represented by a union. Since we wanted to be able to communicate with our supporters, in our case we also asked for their phone numbers and email addresses on the cards. But all you really need is a name, signature, and date.

How do you get workers to sign cards? Beyond speaking with workers, you'll also want to invest in other written materials that clearly spell out your goals and values. Do you have a mission statement that you can pass out at events? Pamphlets? In our case, Chris put together our original TCOEW mission statement, using some of his previous speeches from rallies and focusing on the fact that we were fighting to protect the working class. All these materials should give workers a sense of what your goals are and inspire them to want to sign an authorization card.

According to federal labor law, organizers need to get at least **30 percent of their workplace** to sign authorization cards to be able to hold an election. These are fundamental to your campaign. Without signed cards, there can be no election and no union.

Originally, we had planned to unionize all four Amazon buildings on Staten Island: JFK8, the largest fulfillment center in New York state; LDJ5, a sorting center for merchandise; DYY6, a delivery station; and DYX2, a distribution center, which closed in 2023. If you combine the workers in all four buildings, there are about eight thousand people. That meant we would need at least twenty-four hundred signed authorization cards.

Once you have enough signed cards, the next step is to submit them to the NLRB, where they're tallied and verified to make sure that at least 30 percent of employees have signed. This is where it can get tricky, since companies play with these numbers to buy time. When we turned in our cards, which tallied up to more than two thousand signatures, Amazon, to my knowledge, inflated the employment numbers they gave to the NLRB, saying there were eight thousand workers at JFK8 *alone*, which meant we'd need to gather more signatures to reach 30 percent. Those of us who are inside the building knew that didn't sound right, but we went back out anyway and managed to get six hundred more signatures. Sure enough, when we asked for proof of employment numbers, Amazon submitted an old payroll list of associates, which we were able to see. We easily identified plenty of workers who no longer worked for the company. We saw that the real number was about five thousand workers, or sixty-five hundred including seasonal and part-time workers. We'd had more than enough signatures all along.

It's difficult to know exactly how many workers are in any building. In Amazon's case it's even harder, given that the burn rate is so high, with more than 150 percent turnover. Someone who signs a card could be gone the very next day. That's why, even though you only need 30 percent, it's safer to shoot for 50 to 70 percent of employees to sign cards. We figured out that at JFK8, getting 70 percent of workers to sign would mean collecting around 170 signed cards every single day. That's a lot of one-on-one conversations. How are you going to get the opportunity to talk to so many people in a day while still doing your job?

This is another reason that knowing your rights and having a labor lawyer are so important.

During a union drive, you can't ask workers to sign cards in workspaces during work hours. Instead, **they need to sign up in nonwork areas, at nonworking times**. This means you'll have to wait until they're on break or outside the facility. It's critical to figure out where you can have the most access to workers when they're not working.

The answer in our case, and maybe in yours, was the break rooms.

Later in the book, I'll talk about the crucial importance of break rooms and the battles we fought to get access to them during nonworking hours. Without the break rooms, I don't believe we would have been able to get enough signed authorization cards to file for an election. The bus stop was key, but that was off grounds. To be successful, you also need to be seen and heard inside the building. For us, the break room was the place where we made this happen.

Nothing goes forward without authorization cards. So make sure you're following the rules and that you get them signed.

Building a Social Media Campaign and Digital Presence

In the past, traditional media outlets—newspapers, magazines, television—determined what was "news." As I'm sure you know, that's no longer true. Nowadays, activists, organizers, experts, influencers, elected officials, and high-profile personalities of all kinds can change national conversations simply by logging on to their social media accounts. Organizers can use this shift in how media works to our advantage. For the ALU, our digital platform was our primary form of publicity and creating awareness.

Building **a powerful online presence** is another one of those steps that needs to happen even before you start your campaign. We hadn't had a vote yet, and didn't even have authorization cards signed, when we set up our first Amazon Labor Union page. In other words, **we created an ALU website before there was even an official ALU**. The fact that we hadn't had a vote yet didn't really matter. We claimed the domain name and the digital space. If you want to be taken seriously by your fellow coworkers and by the general public, you need to have that kind of vision and confidence. People need to be able to find you right away with a quick Google search. They need to be able to learn what you're all about and make sure you're legit. Make your announcements there right from the start. Get your TikTok, Instagram, and X accounts up as soon as possible.

Our first website wasn't too good. It was bland. But a website doesn't need to be fancy in the beginning. It just needs to have the basics of a landing page. It needs to tell people what the union is about, what you've done so far, why you're organizing, and what your goal is. It should also have some pictures of actual workers who are current employees. Most importantly, it should have a way to get in touch. Whether you provide an email or phone number or both, people need to have direct access to your leadership team.

What if you're not great at posting on social media? It doesn't matter, as long as you're capturing everything. Every organizer should be hands-on in creating content and contributing. You probably won't have a dedicated IT or social media team yet. That's something you'll need to build later. So at the start, everyone in the union should be thinking about taking videos and photos at every opportunity and posting constantly, 24-7. Every rally, every barbecue, every dispute inside the building—all these events need to be **documented and shared**.

In terms of content, we all know that visuals are better than text. So we posted images of the ALU talking to workers, giving out literature, and listening to music at group gatherings. Anything and everything. Images are so important, and videos are the best kind of content you can offer. In today's online environment, these need to be short, thirty seconds or less usually, to be effective. So many of our quick, casual TikTok videos went viral. They got millions of views, instantly and overnight.

But we also worked to create spectacles when we could. There was the time we built a guillotine outside Jeff Bezos's Washington, DC, mansion. That was a statement that we wanted to make after we read reports that Bezos's personal wealth had surpassed $200 billion. Those images went viral on social media, which meant that we also got important coverage from traditional media. Our actions outside Bezos's various homes around the country led to news coverage from many of the major outlets like Fox, Bloomberg, CBS, and others.

Another example of a viral moment was when a fire broke out inside JFK8 in 2022. Workers captured video of the flames on their phones because, legally, we're able to do that in an unsafe work environment. That *really* got people's attention. We also used social media to "out" the union busters Amazon hired to intimidate workers as they roamed around the building. We put up pictures and videos of them on our accounts explaining what they were doing.

Before Covid, it was Amazon policy that workers had to keep our phones in our lockers. After Covid hit, however, and people needed to stay in touch with family members, we were able to get them back. When the pandemic was over, Amazon tried to take them away again, but there was too much backlash from workers. This continues to be an advantage for us and can be one for you, too. Having **phones nearby at all times** means you won't miss an opportunity to document wrongdoing and spread the word online. Of course you want to get as much exposure as you can. But it's also important to keep in mind that even if the content you're creating doesn't go viral, it's still critical to keep a visual record of everything that takes place before, during, and after union drives. You may not get national visibility or a crazy number of followers, but that doesn't mean your campaign isn't effectively bringing about change inside your company.

I usually post my updates on Instagram, which is where I'm most active. But everyone should be thinking about posting on as many platforms as they can. In addition to us founders, we later brought on Cassio Mendoza, a salt (more on that term later) from Los Angeles who had a background in production and film. We met him when we were protesting outside Bezos's Beverly Hills mansion, and he soon came on board. He was willing to relocate to Staten Island for the campaign, and we welcomed him in. He helped with press communications and spearheaded our TikTok campaign, co-creating some of our most viral videos.

There's one of us giving out pizza in the Amazon parking lot, talking to workers and dancing to Outkast's "Hey Ya!" It has more than a million views. Another video shows an Amazon employee getting called out for illegally taking down union literature. She's nervous and won't give us her last name. She just keeps saying, "Tammy. Tammy. Tammy," in this really high-pitched voice. Right away, after we confronted her, she said she was going to put the literature "right back" and "thank you so much." Those kinds of videos really give people an insider's view into the dynamics between workers and management.

Later, when filmmakers Stephen Maing, Brett Story, and Martin Dicicco started making the ALU documentary, *Union*, it really helped to tell our story and get the word out to the public. The film was on the Oscar short list for Best Documentary in 2024. Most unionization efforts won't be the subject of an Oscar-short-listed documentary! It served as proof that capturing your work matters and can lead to unexpected support.

Some videos are more practically significant than others. Anything illegal, such as retaliation from management, absolutely must be documented. One of our most viral and important videos captured just such a situation.

It happened in late February 2022, about a month before the vote. We were outside passing out food at lunchtime—grilled chicken, pasta platters, and African rice. Chris

Smalls had come to deliver the food, and I was outside talking to him when, suddenly, the general manager and assistant general manager came out and tried to kick him off the property. About six police and security cars pulled up, also trying to arrest other organizers. A worker named Karen Ponce, who's in the ALU and was on our executive board, recorded a short video as she was running out of the break room to see what was going on. She sent it to me, and I immediately put it up on TikTok and Instagram. It got 16,000 views. Later, there were other videos from the same day that got as many as 206,000 views.

People viewing the footage were shocked to see, most likely for the first time, how Amazon was having people arrested, literally, for passing out food. Visitors and guests come to the property all the time to deliver food. As Chris said in the video, why wasn't he like any other visitor or guest who was allowed to be there? Instead, they put their hands on him and treated him like a criminal. The impact of this video on public support for our cause was immense.

We like to say that day was another moment when Amazon lost the election, right then and there. People were outraged. It was another retaliatory move that went poorly for them. Firing Chris and leaking a racist memo to thousands of people was one. Then, arresting him and other organizers on camera for bringing food was another. We got a flood of supporters just from the food incident alone, in addition to receiving tons of coverage in traditional media outlets.

You never can predict where content and coverage will

take you. Supporters and fans show up when your movement becomes part of the national spotlight—or even when it reaches only a particular community, on a local level. Some of these people genuinely want to help. Others might have different motives, even if they seem to be on your side.

In September 2020, a former Amazon employee named Connor Spence showed up at our TCOEW Labor Day rally in New York City, where we planned to march to Jeff Bezos's East Side mansion. Connor had been working at the Amazon facility EWR4 in Robbinsville (where I used to work) before being fired. He said he was fired for running out of "unpaid time off" (UPT) but I felt that something about his story never quite added up. He drove about two hours to Manhattan all the way from Toms River in New Jersey, where he was living at the time, to attend our rally.

This was the first time we'd ever seen Connor. He came up to us and said to Chris, "Hey, I saw you guys on TV. I want to get involved." We were like, "Okay, cool." But when he shook my hand, I noticed that he was so nervous his whole body was shaking. One thing I learned as a child was that you could tell a lot about someone by the way they shook your hand. That should have been a red flag to me right there.

We still have a picture of Connor, where he took his place marching in the front row with the four of us on that same day. We were all wearing our black TCOEW shirts except him, because he was new. Still he was there, holding up what Jordan likes to call, jokingly, a little homemade ninety-nine-cent-store cardboard sign.

Connor ended up becoming very active in our movement, helping with our Twitter account. Eventually, we made him ALU treasurer. But his story took an unfortunate turn down the road, which I'll talk about later in the book.

No Such Thing as Private Accounts

To reach the widest possible audience, your digital content not only should appear on the union's website and official social media pages; it should be on every single organizer's personal accounts as well. Use everything you have. Chris alone currently has around 75,000 followers on Instagram, which is even more than our official ALU account. Before TCOEW and the ALU, he started out with about 130.

I also try to stay connected to every supporter I meet, both inside the building and around the country. I add as many workers as I can to my Instagram so that I can keep up with what they're doing, and so they can do the same. Also, I like to personally message people when there's an event or an update they should know about. If I want to make sure the night-shift workers at JFK8 get a message, I might wake up at 3:00 a.m. to get it out. Organizing is something you do 24-7. Be ready for a crazy sleep pattern. Me, I'm always up.

Every member of your team should also be working hard to connect with people daily and expand the union's reach. In fact, my personal account *is* my union account. I don't use a separate personal platform. I feel like keeping it all in one place is most effective for me, in terms of my energy and time management. The way I see it, why would I need a "private" account, which is never "private" anyway?

If anyone still has any doubts about "privacy" when it comes to organizing, or life today, they should look at a recent study that came out in March 2025. It was done by Teke Wiggin, a graduate student in the Department of Sociology at Northwestern University. It was significant because it was the first in-depth academic investigation into how Amazon uses algorithms as a union-busting tool. Wiggin interviewed dozens of Amazon workers and received NLRB data through the Freedom of Information Act as he put together his research. In conclusion, he described Amazon as a "despot" that uses "plantation-style management" to track workers, especially those at the Bessemer, Alabama, facility.

He documented Amazon's surveillance program, which kept track of all the various social media groups workers had formed to discuss grievances, some of them supposedly private. "More than 43 Facebook groups" were monitored by Amazon to look for complaints, planned strikes, or protests, according to Wiggin. Keep in mind that all employees have the company's A to Z app on our phones. It's something we rely on to find our shifts, overtime, pay, and other crucial information. That means that Amazon automatically has access to our personal devices. It's critical that every organizer recognize this important truth: there is no such thing as privacy when it comes to your digital signature and presence.

Pros and Cons of Different Platforms

Which social media accounts do you really need? The short answer is **all of them**. Or as many as you can realistically maintain. I know that isn't always possible, though, which means you'll have to prioritize, especially in the beginning. Think about which audience you need to reach first. For us, TikTok and Instagram were musts. They are where our core base is, in terms of the mostly young workforce at Amazon. More than half of Amazon workers nationwide are between the ages of twenty and thirty, and they stay on these sites.

Even though a platform like X attracts an older demographic, you still need to be there, too. That's where you're still going to reach other labor unions, attorneys, politicians, educators, and more established activists, despite the changes since Elon Musk took over. At the time of writing, our X account has the largest number of followers, at about 109,000, compared to our Instagram, which has 58,000, and our TikTok with 64,000. Even though our core audience lives on those last two platforms, which is also where we've had a lot of viral successes, we've reached more people overall, and from a wider variety of industries, on X, especially back when it was Twitter.

If there's a platform that we didn't pay much attention to, I'd have to say that it was Facebook. To me, Facebook always felt out of touch and not useful. It's known as an "older person's" platform, but I've also learned that Facebook's strength is that it reaches multiple generations at once. Even though it has a reputation for being irrelevant to young people, its largest demographic (31 percent) is still twenty-five- to thirty-year-olds. It's still a platform that should be included and one that, in retrospect, fell through the cracks for us. Every movement will have different needs and strategies, and different audiences to prioritize. But in a fractured media age, cross-posting across as much social media as possible is absolutely vital.

Raising Money

It goes without saying that you will need to have large amounts of money to invest in your campaign. Everything starts to add up quickly. We spent about $100,000–$120,000 in the months before the election. That went to the huge barbecues we held at the bus stop to recruit and engage workers, as well as ALU T-shirts, all of our union literature we distributed, and authorization cards. We also bought a Chevy Suburban that cost about five thousand dollars and served as storage for all the equipment, merchandise, barbecue supplies, and tents.

For us the fundraising platform that made the most sense to use as we started out was GoFundMe. We promoted this account constantly, on every social media platform, on our ALU Twitter account, our ALU Instagram account, and our personal pages. **You can't be shy about asking for money.** No one is going to know about your campaign, or that you need funding, unless you make it known. At first, things were slow, but we kept promoting our GoFundMe everywhere until we started to build support.

One of our videos caught the attention of More Perfect Union, which is a nonprofit journalism organization that focuses on union campaigns and the working class. They pushed our GoFundMe a few times on their Twitter account, which was huge for us. I believe a few thousand dollars came in from that alone.

We gave our T-shirts away to workers for free, of course, but we also sold them to supporters outside of Amazon to raise money. They cost about ten dollars each to make, and we priced them for around thirty dollars via our website. People loved our merchandise. The front of the shirt said "ALU" in black, bold letters. On the back they said either, "When We Fight, We Win," or, "Recognize ALU." Some of the shirts also had an entire list of our demands on the back. We marketed our movement constantly by wearing our ALU merchandise to every speaking event, every break room organizing meeting, and even to award ceremonies. It was like our uniform. We wore it with pride.

Overall, we raised around half a million dollars during

our leadership, but most of that didn't come until after we'd won the election. We had very little money on hand when we were campaigning and were barely getting by week to week. In fact, before the election, we were down to something like $2.50 in our account.

In this sense, we were disappointed by the support of other, traditional unions. None of them made any kind of major financial contribution before the election. Unite Here! Local 100 in Manhattan allowed us to use their office space for a few weeks to do our phone bank, which was helpful. But I can't think of any major contributors.

After we won, funding started to flow in more regularly. The American Federation of Teachers (AFT) showed up for us big-time. They donated $250,000. That's how we were able to get a two-year lease on fifteen thousand square feet of office space on Staten Island. Our rent was $12,500 a month and we were finally able to hire fifteen staff members, including some students from CUNY who stayed on after their internships were over. A few other unions donated as well. Our biggest individual donor was YouTube streamer Hasan Piker, who gave us around $175,000–$200,000.

For the doubters and the skeptics, it's important for organizers to be clear: **No one at the ALU was making any kind of wild compensation on our payroll**. These were modest salaries and stipends that allowed the movement to keep running, even to our highest officers and executive board members.

After we won the election, our GoFundMe account had

to be transitioned into a public support campaign because we were now a public entity. After the NLRB stated we didn't have enough cards signed, we knew it made more sense for us to strictly focus on JFK8 so that two thousand cards signed would be enough to get an election. We signed up with Action Network, which is an extension of ActBlue, a nonprofit fundraising platform for progressive activism and causes. During his time as president, Chris sent out an email every week to around one hundred thousand people, and we received solid, recurring donations. When things were still "peachy creamy," as he puts it, we sometimes were able to bring in as much as thirty thousand dollars a month.

However, this was pennies compared to what we needed to go up against a $2 trillion company like Amazon. Our legal fees alone were more than we were raising. A single ULP case involving one person could cost anywhere from two thousand dollars to ten thousand dollars. We were fighting more than 175 of those cases.

When you're starting out, it's important to understand that **funding is probably the biggest challenge of all** in being an independent union. Even with a dynamic leader like Chris, who was able to express our struggle so well and move huge audiences emotionally, we were always in the red. The ALU is still in the red today, and it will continue to be in the red for as long as it keeps representing thousands of workers inside JFK8 with no contract and with no union dues coming in.

We were a grassroots, worker-led movement that was just

two years old when we won the election. We were never a big, established, traditional union. People seem to forget this or misunderstand it. The expectations outsiders sometimes had for us, right out of the gate, were insanely unrealistic. Did we fall behind on our bills at times? Of course we did. But we kept on doing the best we could with what we had, and somehow, we made it work. Keep raising money!

Using Traditional Media to Your Advantage

I talked earlier about social media, which is crucial to your campaign. But it's a mistake to think that journalism and traditional news outlets don't matter. If you think about it, a lot of what people are reacting to on social media comes from reporting done by major news outlets like CNN, *The New York Times*, Fox, *Fortune*, *The Wall Street Journal*, and others.

News also comes from *The Washington Post*, although Jeff Bezos owns that now, too, which has begun to impact what they cover in a huge way. Just look at what happened in February 2025 when Bezos sent out a memo to his staff outlining his change in the direction of the company. "We are going to be writing every day in support and defense of two pillars: personal liberties and free markets," he wrote. He acknowledged that this was a "significant shift" and ended the memo by saying, "I'm confident that free markets and personal liberties are right for America. I also believe these viewpoints are underserved in the current market of ideas and news opinion." He made it very clear who he planned to serve going forward. Several high-profile editors resigned in disgust.

Still, regardless of the political slant of traditional media outlets, organizers need to know how to reach out to them, even if it's Fox News or the *Post*, and to work with professional reporters and editors to get their stories told.

At the same time, it's important to know that big-name media attention won't in and of itself create a movement for you. The real work is grassroots, and organizers still need to do the hard work of connecting with workers one by one, every day. We didn't take breaks from organizing even when huge news stories dropped. We never stopped taking direct action: getting cards signed, speaking up at labor events and rallies, filing lawsuits. We used the traditional media as an added plus, to enhance and amplify what we were already doing on the ground.

The most important thing about working with journalists and editors at news outlets is, again, to **start early, long before your campaign begins**. Reach out and let them know you're planning to unionize your workplace. Obviously, you don't want to give away your entire game plan, but you do want to get the word out that something big is about to happen, no matter the size of the company you work for.

I have a good relationship with the reporters I know and always make sure they're aware of what's going on. Those connections are your protection. If you're out there publicly, planning an action, and Amazon tries to fire you, it won't be a good look for the company if the press gets wind of it. Your employer may think twice about trying to retaliate against you once you've demonstrated you know how to reach the press.

How do you capture the attention of journalists and editors at news outlets? Media professionals cover all kinds of stories, 24-7. You need to be able to explain **what makes your story stand out**. There's a saying in journalism that "dog bites man" isn't a news story. That happens every day. But "man bites dog"? *That's* a news story! What happened? What made him do it? Readers and viewers are curious because it's so unusual. Now they want to know more.

For us, we did outrageous things that would stand out, like building a guillotine outside Jeff Bezos's Washington, DC, mansion. Even the celebrity gossip outlet TMZ covered those events, and globally, we were covered from as far away as *The Japan Times*. Our philosophy from the beginning was that unorthodox, nontraditional organizing is the key to our success. We were a whole new wave of activists, and we were not doing things the same old way; that applied to publicity and word spreading, too. We weren't following the standard union playbook. To make a difference, you need to be different.

Sometimes there are individual reporters who will follow your actions regularly, and they can be huge assets. Maybe their beat is business, labor, or social justice, so they'll take consistent interest in whatever you're doing once you get going. In the best cases, these reporters won't just interview you once. They'll track your story and keep updating it whenever something new happens. **Those are the reporters, whether national or local, you need to get to know well and communicate regularly with.** Make sure you take the time to research reporters you think will have a particular interest in your movement based on what they've covered in the past.

Jodi Kantor at *The New York Times* has followed us since the beginning. Her first story about Amazon came out in 2015. She was the journalist I talked to most often. We had in-depth conversations about what was happening inside the warehouse. What impressed me most about Jodi's reporting was that she took her time with the coverage and really provided us with in-depth knowledge we previously hadn't had access to. In this way, serious reported journalism can be helpful not just for publicity but also because you're able to utilize what these reporters discover.

For example, I learned about Amazon's 150 percent turnover rate from Jodi's article, "The Amazon Customers Don't See," which came out in June 2021. That story also talked about how Black and brown workers were less likely to get promoted than white workers at Amazon. It was part of a deep investigation into the company that *The New York Times* did that year. They even found out something that was particularly shocking to me: apparently, Amazon's HR department was stretched so thin that they were firing employees by mistake.

Most of the workers I know don't pay much attention to

what's being reported in *The New York Times* or *The Washington Post*. It's hard for someone who barely has time to take a lunch break to really sit down and digest an entire article. They're more focused on quick bites that show up on their social media feeds. But in the case of Jodi's report, I thought the information was so important that I took the time to print out key sections of the article and pass copies around to workers.

Another example of how journalism can be critical to your cause was from a June 2022 story that came out on a technology news site called *Recode* (which is now part of *Vox*). Those reporters were able to get their hands on a leaked internal memo from Amazon that talked about how worried the company was about their own high turnover rate. They were slash-and-burning their way through employees at a rate that was nearly triple that of the overall transportation and warehouse sector. "If we continue business as usual," the memo said, "Amazon will deplete the available labor supply in the U.S. network by 2024." That was remarkable to read—and critical material to back up our fight for workers' rights.

These traditional outlets have provided key intel and insight for us. We know about conditions firsthand from our experiences, but we don't have the kind of resources that are needed to do in-depth, factual investigations of the company. As it turns out, we discovered through many of these articles that we were often completely in the dark about what was happening right under our noses at JFK8.

3.

The ALU's Secret Sauce

Our Secret Sauce: Independence

In early 2021, as we continued building our campaign, we kept a close watch on workers' efforts to organize an Amazon facility in Bessemer, Alabama. The whole country did. It was the first time that any Amazon facility would have a vote for a union, so with that alone, Bessemer had already made history. Their movement was endorsed by national labor groups and celebrity politicians like Senator Bernie Sanders and House Representative Alexandria Ocasio-Cortez. They even received a statement of support from President Joe Biden. But, in the end, the campaign failed, and in March 2021 workers at Bessemer voted against the union. This setback taught us important lessons as we started to put together our own plan for JFK8. So before I talk about our secret sauce within the ALU, I want to discuss what we learned from Bessemer.

When Chris and I first heard workers were organizing there in early 2021, we were excited and wanted to know more. We decided to make the sixteen-hour drive down on Valentine's Day weekend, along with a few other workers, to check it out and offer our support. The whole experience was transformative and taught us so much about what to do and what not to do.

One of the first things we learned on our visit was about basic logistics. We discovered that since Amazon typically owns the roads leading to their facilities, as well as the parking lots, organizers need to find somewhere else, somewhere neutral, to talk to workers. For Bessemer, this spot became a nearby Circle K gas station where many workers would go eat because everything inside Amazon was so expensive.

We headed over to the Circle K, excited to meet with their team. But when we got there at around 6:00 a.m., we saw something that we never expected to see. Workers were going in and out of the gas station, but the organizers were asleep in their cars! They were supposed to be out there talking to people! Obviously, they were tired. I get that. But you still have to engage somehow, or what's the point of even being out there at all? (Later, when we had our own campaign, we also often slept outside, in a tent, but we set our alarms so we could meet the night-shift workers as they came out of the building.)

When we got to the gas station, Chris and I started asking workers if they knew about the union drive. We were disappointed by the fact that so many of them said they didn't. That was eye-opening to us. Bessemer was making national news at that time. It was in the headlines. And yet, here their organizers were, preparing for an election where most of the workers we talked to didn't even know about it. That was a very serious problem.

Another issue, from my point of view, was that the RWDSU, a large traditional union with one hundred thousand members, was leading the movement at Bessemer. The two main employee organizers inside the building were

Darryl Richardson, who was also a pastor, and Jennifer Bates, who was a member of the United Steelworkers union (USW) for ten years before coming to Amazon. Jennifer has told me that the union had other leaders within the warehouse in every department (except on the night shift), but to be honest, when we were there, we didn't see that. Instead, it seemed like the two of them were the only voices being heard talking to the media, and the only public faces of the movement.

This wasn't a good look. It made it seem like only two workers inside a building were trying to organize seven thousand others! Our group took note of this, and it became really clear to us that we had to have many, many more workers on the inside helping to not only spread the word but also be forward facing with the media. A team of insiders needed to be in the building passing out literature and counteracting the company's anti-union scare tactics. And they needed to be visible to the world, not hidden away from the press, so that the workers inside knew and understood that there was representation from every department in the public sphere, and that as a result their voices would be heard.

I've said earlier that one of our mistakes at JFK8 was that we didn't have union leadership in every department, on every shift. I wish we'd been able to have more leaders on the inside before starting our campaign. It's important for me to say that openly, so that other organizers understand the huge impact it can make on a campaign when two or three workers seem to be isolated and out there on their own as the only voices for a much larger movement.

Another disappointment we felt at Bessemer was that the white leadership of the RWDSU really didn't want our help. They let us know in no uncertain terms that we weren't needed there. One of them even said that our being there might "intimidate" workers. Why was that? Because we were Black? Because Chris had been fired? We weren't sure.

Still we felt that there was a cultural division at play, with much of the RWDSU leadership being from the South and us being from the North. They basically sent us on our way. So off we went back to New York. That, to me, seemed like a missed opportunity for the Bessemer folks. We never even got to meet with the two main leaders inside the building—Darryl Richardson and Jennifer Bates—both of whom are Black.

What was most troubling was that the actions of the RWDSU leaders seemed to be based on fear and what-ifs, and not on evidence or engagement. How do you know what workers will feel, or think, until you talk with them? Until you have a chance to connect? I believe our group could have helped tip the scales for them, if only they had been more open and less fearful.

It was no surprise to us that Amazon won that election in a landslide vote. The organizing team at Bessemer wasn't ready for a behemoth like Amazon. The NLRB later ruled that the company had interfered illegally with the election, which also wasn't a surprise, and ordered that a new election take place. But there's always a problem with getting a second vote, especially at big corporations. By the time you get it, it's taken so long, and worker turnover is so high, that a company like Amazon has managed to destroy all the momentum you built.

In 2022, Bessemer managed to hold a second vote, which was indecisive, meaning that 993 people voted "no" and 875 voted "yes," but more than 400 additional votes were contested and 59 were considered void. The NLRB will need to determine whether those contested votes will be counted. Until then, the outcome of that election is yet to be determined.

Nothing else happened there for a long time. Then, in November 2024, a federal judge ruled that Bessemer would be able to hold a third election. As of this writing, they're still waiting to find out when that will happen. Given the lack of support for the NLRB under President Trump, it's not likely to be anytime soon.

But it's not over for Bessemer. After the first vote, Amazon offered a small concession to workers: a raise of $1.00–$1.50 an hour. That brought starting wages to about $16 an hour in a state that still has a shameful minimum wage of $7.25 and still doesn't believe workers are entitled to any kind of paid breaks. (Thankfully, federal law offers guidelines for paid breaks of at least five to twenty minutes.)

Since then, Jennifer Bates has told me that their campaign started a conversation in the Deep South that hadn't happened in generations, and that has made a lot of people more aware of the importance of unions not only there but nationwide. She thinks this awareness has been their biggest victory. I think she's right. Being the first Amazon facility in the country to have a union vote has already made a huge impact.

Two of Jennifer's daughters work at Mercedes-Benz in Alabama, where there is much more talk now about organizing. In 2024 more than forty-five hundred workers at a plant in Vance, Alabama, voted on whether to join the United Auto Workers. The union lost that battle, but it was close. Even after all the company's intimidation tactics and firings, only 56 percent of workers voted against the union.

Just the fact that 30 percent of workers had signed union authorization cards, even before a vote, was enough to make Mercedes offer some workers a two-dollar increase in hourly wages, while also restructuring their wage system to make it easier to reach higher wage levels.

Support for unions is also more prevalent among coal mine workers in Alabama than it was before the Bessemer vote. In 2021, about one thousand mine workers went on strike for nearly two years—the longest strike in Alabama history. They didn't get a contract, unfortunately, but their courageous mass action shows that the conversation is spreading. I know that with continued organizing inside, and with ongoing solidarity and mass actions across the country, Bessemer will make their comeback.

After seeing what happened in Alabama during that

first campaign, we at JFK8 knew one thing for sure: we *had* to be independent. But let me be clear: This may not be true for everyone. For some workplaces, affiliation is absolutely the best choice. I'll discuss the pros and cons in more detail later, but for now, let's just say that as founders of the ALU, we needed to build our own union, by ourselves, from the ground up. This route won't work for everyone. Being independent is always going to be more difficult than having a large traditional union behind you. It means, first of all, that you will have to raise all of your own money.

But autonomy comes with benefits. The ALU could do things exactly how we wanted, with no one forcing us to follow old-school rules and hierarchies. We were nothing like traditional unions and didn't intend to use their playbook. In twenty-nine years, nobody had ever taken on Amazon and won. We had to do it in a way that had never been seen before, with a different, scrappier type of commitment.

Our idea to set up at the bus stop is an example of how we used our autonomy to shift the status quo. That first day out, we used $150 from our GoFundMe account to buy two tables, four chairs, and a tent from Walmart. Later, we put up a heating lamp with "ALU" written across it in black duct tape. Chris and I stayed out there for more than three hundred days and nights talking to workers. That was hard. What other union president and vice president camp out overnight for nearly a year? I remember our cofounder Gerald Bryson once said, "It takes heart and soul to do this." We had to believe that organizing was about service to others, not to ourselves. No one should get involved if they don't truly believe those words.

Four Friends and a Lifelong Bond

Our team of four cofounders came together organically; most of us were already friends. Jordan and Gerald lived in the same building on Staten Island, and they met because Jordan played basketball with Gerald's older son, who was in an overseas league. One day, Jordan told Gerald that he worked in Robotics at Amazon. That was all Gerald needed to hear. He applied to work at JFK8, too.

Every worker at Amazon has a four-week learning curve for each department they're trained in. During this time, workers aren't supposed to be retrained unless they make quality errors. When Gerald was first hired, the system said he miscounted items during his initial training, so he was put on probation. As an ambassador, I was the person assigned to retrain him. So I was friends with both Gerald and Jordan even before I met Chris. Later, Chris became a direct supervisor to me and Gerald. From the start, Amazon really wanted to fire Gerald. He was always outspoken about the safety conditions at JFK8, which made him a threat. Meanwhile, I had my own problems with John Stanton, as I've explained earlier, so we were both frustrated.

Once Gerald and I were working with Chris, though,

we got some relief. Chris didn't go for any of that. He knew how Amazon disrespected people, and he wasn't going to allow them to do that to us. He took us under his wing and helped us all thrive. We became the best team in the building. Our numbers set records.

During the pandemic, having to go to work in those conditions, the bonds between the four of us strengthened. We became closer as we started to organize and spend more time hanging out together outside of work. And that closeness is what helped make us good organizers.

The three of us took Jordan, the baby of our group, to his first nightclub when he turned twenty-one. That's a story that never gets old, and we will never let him live it down. We were in the car on the way to the club, a place called Lit 21 in New Jersey. I guess none of us had really thought about what Jordan was wearing. When we got there, a security guard took one look at Jordan and told him there was no way he was getting inside with sweatpants on. So we had to drive all the way back home to Staten Island, about thirty minutes away, so Jordan could change into some cargo pants. We lost an hour and a half at the club because of that. To this day, we'll never stop clowning Jordan about it. That's the kind of thing that helps us stay close, those funny moments and memories we share with one another.

We also joke *a lot* about New Jersey versus Staten Island. Chris and I clown on Jordan and Gerald, saying that we "saved" them from Staten Island. We call ourselves the big brothers (even though Gerald is the oldest, at fifty-nine) because we feel like we had to come from New Jersey to rescue them and take care of them. Gerald describes himself as "a young older dude," anyways. Chris and I like to call him "Lil' Bro" as part of the joke.

We've been through a lot together. Through it all, we always find time to laugh. I think that's the best thing we have going for ourselves. It's part of the glue that holds us together. Jordan is probably the biggest jokester among us. He likes to clown on Bezos, too, talking about how little he is. Bezos is five feet seven, and Jordan is six feet two. He likes to joke about how Bezos went into space in his little "penis rocket." It's both sad and funny how Bezos thanked Amazon employees for sending him to space. "Man, that's like telling us, 'Thank you for letting me rob you!'" Jordan always says.

It's true. It reminds me of when Amazon ended its two-dollars-an-hour wage increases at Bessemer during the pandemic, and then turned around, that same summer of 2020 when workers were struggling and made a $10 million donation to social justice organizations like the NAACP and the Brennan Center as proof of their support for the Black Lives Matter movement. Even though their Black employees were struggling more than ever.

Going up against a powerful corporation like Amazon is incredibly draining. You need to have those breaks to laugh, and you need to have friends and fellow workers to laugh with. We all need outlets for release. It's the only way to keep your sanity.

On Sundays we'll be at one of our houses, watching

football and talking about stuff outside of organizing. When I was still in New Jersey, Gerald and Jordan would drive from Staten Island and we would meet up at my house in Elizabeth. Once we were able to purchase the ALU Chevy Suburban, Chris, who was in Hackensack, would drive over, too, taking the New Jersey Turnpike to get to Elizabeth.

In 2023, I moved to Staten Island and became roommates with Jordan. We share a two-bedroom apartment in the same building where he and Gerald already lived, so now, we meet up either there or at Gerald's. Both Gerald and Chris are single parents. Gerald sometimes babysits his two grandsons now, too. They talk about dad and family stuff. Honestly, we talk about everything. It's like a venting session.

Having that foundation is so important. Every serious organizer needs **a core team** that you can be honest with and let everything out alongside. Because the world will try to divide you, and you should be prepared emotionally for that. Everyone needs a strong support system. Not only will a company like Amazon try to tear you apart, but so will other organizers, the public, and the press. It happened to us, and we had to learn from experience how to protect ourselves and our bond; our core, the connection between us, isn't going anywhere. That stays strong.

How do we do it?

First, **communication** is the most important thing. In any group dynamic, there's always going to be some tension. The four of us are on a group chat where we stay in contact. If it's something serious, we'll do a group FaceTime as well. The most important thing is that we stay real, and that means honest and truthful. We're open and tell one another how we feel. Even if we stay mad at one another for a few days over a disagreement, that's okay. We get through it, and we move on. Because like Gerald once put it, "We either gon' go down together, or rise up together." Any petty differences between us we just need to get over. That's a pact that we have.

Second, we're **loyal** to one another. Chris was talking to a reporter recently, and he told her he wouldn't even be here if it weren't for me. The reporter was like, "Really?" And Chris responded like, "Wait. No. Seriously. You need to understand what I mean. This man literally picked me up for work when I had no car. He drove me to work every day when I was *his* supervisor. He kept me employed long before we even walked out of that building." It was true. Without a car, Chris's commute from New Jersey was about three hours each way. He had to take a bus, then a train to Manhattan, and then the ferry to Staten Island.

He went on to describe the loyalty, friendship, and brotherhood that we have, saying to the reporter how our bond is forever. Those words really moved me. Chris gets most of the media attention, and he should. He was our president and the public face of our movement. But I also know that he respects me and knows that I have my own voice, too. All of us do. That's what keeps us strong. The four of us put a huge value on each of our individual strengths.

Organizing from the Inside

Up until now we've discussed everything from how to know if you need a union and learning your federal, state, and company laws, to labor lawyers, authorization cards, social media, and money. Now it's time to get into the actual organizing, and that begins inside. As I discuss throughout this book, one of the lessons we learned was that some crucial steps need to happen even before you officially begin your campaign. Again, you want to get educated about basic labor laws before you begin and about the policies within your workplace. You also want to set up a basic website and social media accounts. Likewise, when organizing from the inside, you ideally want to establish leaders in every department, and on every shift, before going public to get workers to sign authorization cards.

A lot of my story is defined by the fact that I was able to be inside the building throughout our campaign as an Amazon employee. All successful labor movements have one crucial fact in common: they're **led by organizers on the inside**. Workers like me with deep experience and seniority know all the ins and outs of the company, as well as its weaknesses.

Organizing from the inside means a lot of things. It means being on the job, inside the facility. It also means having leaders in more than one department and on multiple shifts. It means empowering people you know to be a chairperson, a vice chair, a recording secretary, or a shop steward, and helping to build that leadership structure. It's also about **leading by example**. Do people see you on the job, going hard, wearing your union T-shirts, and being outspoken? If someone is afraid to speak out, organizers on the inside are there to show them how.

This is why you need leaders in every area and department of your workplace to really be successful. It's something we've had to learn the hard way. At Amazon, there are six main departments: Receive, Stow, Count, Pick, Pack, and Ship Dock. When we started, we had leaders in only three of the six departments: Pick, Pack, and Stow. The others were the great unknown, up for grabs, since no one from the ALU was there, watching to see what was happening and standing up against the anti-union messages. This isn't ideal, since we had no idea how those workers would vote.

As you start to think strategically about organizing, it's also important, no matter where you work, to **understand how each department is structured differently**. Some areas may be easier to organize than others because stations are right next to each other. In my department, for example, I can go talk to a worker in front of me and, boom, have a quick conversation and get right back to work. I can connect with them casually, too, on a lot of other things that have nothing to do with the ALU, just by simply hanging out with them and having more time to get to know one another. At some workplaces, employees don't have that kind of access to one another.

Again, the goal should be to have **at least one leader in**

each department in your workplace. We never quite got there during our campaign, unfortunately, and that was a mistake. I believe we could have gotten more authorization cards signed, much more quickly, if we had established organizers in all six departments of Amazon, and on every single shift, before going public with our campaign. That would have meant delaying a little longer, but it would have been worth it to have the extra strength.

Instead, we had to fully utilize every opportunity we had to get inside the break rooms, where we could talk to workers from all different departments. To do this, you need to plan and be strategic since break time is limited for everyone. In a workplace without break rooms, or with more opportunities to talk casually with your coworkers, it's still critical to find the places within the building to talk safely about organizing. In some cases, that might be the parking lot or a public bench across the street or, as in our case, a bus stop.

Like the departments, break rooms also vary at different workplaces. At JFK8, for example, one of our departments has a small break area that's literally right behind the bathroom. If you want to have an intimate setting with those workers, you need to go there. The main break room, which is farther away, is less intimate. But you can find workers there from many different departments. So the first thing you need to do is **to know who exactly is going to be where and who you most need to talk to**. Then, you need to get down there early so you can set up your table and have your pamphlets and merchandise out and ready to distribute (more on break rooms later on). Don't ever forget that you are legally entitled to distribute pro-union materials, no matter where you work, although it's important to know the specific policies of your workplace. Some companies restrict distribution of all non-work-related materials during working hours and in work areas.

Lessons Learned: Albany

In October 2022, workers at the ALB1 warehouse near Albany, New York, voted 406 to 206 against unionization. It was a brutal defeat. Taking a long, hard look at that campaign taught us a lot about finding potential leaders, organizing from the inside, creating community, and what it really takes to commit to a life of organizing.

Almost from the beginning, there were issues with Heather Goodall, the lead organizer at Albany. First, let me just say that you can't be focused on being in front of the camera above organizing workers. This work isn't about grandstanding or glamour or making a name for yourself. **It's not about your agenda. It's about serving others.** That means getting to know every single one of your workers and what they're going through, so that you can have real, authentic influence inside the building.

Second, **the committee of workers that's doing the job of trying to get cards signed needs to be strong**. They need to constantly engage with workers 24-7. Unfortunately, Heather's worker committee was weak. They only had about six people, in a building with twelve hundred workers, trying to get cards signed. It was also made up of mostly older white women. There were no Black or brown people on that committee at all, and when your workers are mostly Black and brown, it should be common sense that your committee should reflect that.

Third, forming a union isn't a part-time hobby. The way I see it, it's **a full-time calling**. For some workers, their actual livelihood or health are on the line. Helping them, for me, often feels like a life-or-death commitment. If you're really in it, you will lose sleep on a regular basis, trying to figure out how to help those working alongside you. I can't tell you how many times I've tossed and turned at night, thinking about what needed to be done next to keep engaging people and to overcome the union busting. So many people had put their trust in me, and I wasn't about to let them down. I didn't see that commitment or urgency from Heather. I felt like she was a little too well-rested, if you know what I'm saying. There's just no other way to put it.

Workers at Albany faced a lot of union busting, and Amazon broke a lot of laws. That goes without saying; a company like Amazon is going to come for you hard. In fact, they broke so many laws that they ran the risk of the union becoming automatically certified at that warehouse. But that's why you need to be ready to face these hurdles by making sure your leadership is really locked in, and really in it for the right reasons, so that you can mobilize a strong workforce that's able to resist your employer's trickery.

It's rough, looking back, because ultimately, no one can go inside another building and handpick the workers that they think would be good organizers. As I've been saying, the movement needs to come from *inside*. There needs to be an organic connection and energy among workers who know and trust one another to really understand what needs to be done. The mistake that we made with our support of the Albany effort was not catching some of these problems sooner.

We went to Albany so many times. Chris went even more often than I did because I was still working. I think he went around sixteen times and almost got arrested on three of those trips. He sees that situation a little differently than I do. We had a feeling the workers there were going to lose the vote, despite our assistance. There were just too many internal problems with their campaign that we were powerless to fix or to control as outsiders. But Chris believed that we still needed to be there, regardless, because that's what solidarity is all about. On one hand, I understand and respect his point, but on the other hand, we put a lot of effort into a situation that was flawed right from the start. I believe that was our mistake with Albany. We should never have devoted so much time and energy to them once we saw that our interventions weren't helping.

Organizers constantly ask us, "How did you guys do it?" and, "How do we get started?" Workers in these facilities genuinely want our help. But the problem is that a lot of them are just not ready. They think they're going to have a rally here and there and ride the new wave of union organizing. They're picking and choosing bits and pieces of our formula, but they're not really listening. They're not applying the whole strategy, and that's what I saw in Albany.

As an organizer, you need to look in the mirror and ask the hard questions: What are you willing to sacrifice as a leader? Time with your family? Money? Sleep? A social life? Privacy? Too often, Chris and I took the time to have calls with workers from other Amazon buildings or other companies, but once we laid it all out to them, they got cold feet. They backed out, and we never heard from them again. For workplace organizing to truly work, the people inside need to be seriously committed, no matter the outside help, because if they're not, then they're only going to get so far before they hit a wall.

Using Salts

Sometimes, that internal commitment can still be boosted initially from the outside. "Salts" are **union organizers who come from other cities and states to help kick-start campaigns**. They're transplants who have usually been involved with other labor movements before and decide to commit to living and working at your facility. We realized early on that we were going to need the help of salts to organize on the inside. Bringing salts into your support structure within the building is an important and often much-needed step. We were able to find several of them to recruit to apply for jobs at Amazon. Most of the time they simply showed up at our events, or reached out to us directly on social media, saying they wanted to get involved. Some of them were recommended to us by our labor lawyers. These are unpaid volunteers who are dedicated to the organized labor movement and feel called to help. Once hired, salts hold jobs like anyone else and receive pay from the company, of course. But their main purpose is to help organize from within.

Salts are useful because they're people who know something about unions owing to direct experience or from studying organized labor in college. They're effective at speaking with other workers and can create powerful talking points for the cause. We also gave them specific training on how to talk to workers at JFK8, including some of the lingo that we use, and we taught them about routines and customs that are specific to our building.

At the same time, our model was to maintain the real Amazon workers as the key organizers. For us, it was critical to make sure that those workers who had already been in the trenches, and who had survived tough situations at Amazon, were our actual leaders. Also, ours had been a Black-led movement from the start. We tried whenever we could to find salts who looked like the workers, who were mostly Black and brown, and so could connect with them more easily.

The salts are, as Chris puts it, the "help." They should be incognito. Not trying to stand in the limelight. They should not be posting on social media or being interviewed for articles. The salts are there to lay low and help inform workers about the benefits of the union. They're our extra eyes and ears.

Griffin Ritze tried to organize the KCVG in Kentucky, which is Amazon's largest air hub. Ritze was a tug driver there and one of the founders of their movement, which kicked off after Amazon took away additional seasonal peak pay in 2022. They got more than one thousand union cards signed and were close to filing for an election, but not quite close enough. The bottom line was that they didn't have enough organizers inside the building. Also, it didn't help that Ritze was fired in January 2024 after attending "invitation only" captive audience meetings (more on those later).

He was a good organizer and used to call me all the time for advice. But one of the problems they had in Kentucky, in my opinion, was that they relied on too many salts. **Buildings don't get organized from the outside in.** You're never going to win over mostly Black and brown workers by relying on a bunch of outsiders from white leftist groups from other states. Groups like Socialist Alternative and the Democratic Socialists of America (DSA) are amazing organizations, and they can be strong supporters. We had supporters from all kinds of groups, too, like the DSA, the Workers World Party, Extinction Rebellion, and the Sunrise Movement. But if you're relying on these groups to form the core of your team, your movement is never going to feel authentic.

Taking Over the Break Rooms

Whether you've been successful in creating a strong internal leadership structure, with organizers in every department, and on every shift, or whether you're not quite there yet, I can't overemphasize the importance of the break rooms. My experience is with a large warehouse, where being able to congregate in a break room is essential if you're going to reach workers throughout the building. Break rooms are also important in smaller shops, like Starbucks or Trader Joe's, but these situations are different because you may have other opportunities to reach workers throughout the day as well. My sense is that it's logistically easier to organize a store with thirty workers than a warehouse with six thousand people. In our case, how can you reach so many people in the limited time you have? A huge reason we won the election was that we had access to workers inside the facility during their off time. We could go to break rooms to get to know people across departments, gain support, and create a sense of community.

I mentioned earlier that part of my goal was to show workers inside that we weren't scared of Amazon, and that they shouldn't be, either. That's why I wore my TCOEW and ALU T-shirts constantly. It's also why we made ourselves seen and heard in the break rooms. For example, we strung a huge yellow banner across the walls and laid a bright yellow tablecloth out to showcase our pamphlets. That showed that we not only had a right to be there, we also weren't hiding from anyone. Sometimes we even had bullhorns, to make sure people could hear us as we told them to come and learn about the Amazon Labor Union.

The break rooms were a huge battle for us. We knew that elections could live or die on that one question alone: the question of access to workers and having the time and opportunity to talk with them on a regular basis. On June 30, 2022, after we'd won the election, they put new rules in place. Their new policy said: "Effective immediately, only those employees who are scheduled to work are permitted to be in our facilities or on our property. Employees who are scheduled to work may arrive on site up to fifteen minutes before their shift starts. All Employees are expected to clock in/out as usual. Employees are expected to timely depart the site, within fifteen minutes, after their shift ends."

This was flat-out illegal. Workers have the right to organize, as a federally protected activity. If we can't do it during working hours, regardless if we ourselves are scheduled to work, we have a right to use our off time to have free speech conversations with fellow workers on Amazon's premises. But at Amazon and other companies, conversations on the shop floor are severely monitored and discouraged. The entire system is designed to limit interactions, specifically to prevent the kind of fraternizing that can lead to collective advocacy.

In response to Amazon's new restrictions, Chris, Gerald, and I testified in December 2021, along with several other workers, before an administrative law judge at an NLRB hearing. Charges against the new policy had been filed not only by JFK8, but by other Amazon workers at warehouses in Chicago, Minneapolis, and other cities.

We won that battle, thankfully. The NLRB called Amazon's policy "overly broad and discriminatory," and we got a national settlement agreement from Amazon that said they had to rescind the unlawful access policy and that we could organize in the break rooms any day of the week, and not just on days when we clocked in. So even if I wasn't working, I could come to work and sit in the break room all day if I wanted to, giving out literature and talking to other workers.

Outside, at the bus stop, there were some skeptics who didn't believe we even worked for Amazon. They had bought into the company-created lie that the ALU was a "third party." But when they saw us inside the break rooms, some would look surprised and say things like, "Oh, you really *do* work here!" The ruling helped to solidify our place and gave people a feeling of authenticity that was needed.

Not surprisingly, Amazon later went back on their word in violation of the settlement agreement. In June 2022, just a few months after we won, they reverted to saying that off-duty employees couldn't be inside the building, or even in the outdoor areas around the building. The NLRB hit them back the following year with a ruling saying that Amazon had violated the terms of the national agreement by again restricting access to facilities. A default judgment stated that Amazon was unlawfully "interfering with, restraining, and coercing employees" with that policy. Now, the NLRB required them to post public notices inside the building with the following announcement:

FEDERAL LAW GIVES YOU THE RIGHT TO
Form, join, or assist a union
Choose representatives to bargain with us on your behalf
Act together with other employees for your benefit and protection
Choose not to engage in any of these protected activities.

WE WILL NOT create, maintain, or enforce any rules or policies that unlawfully limit your access to exterior, nonwork areas of our facilities.

WE WILL NOT in any like or related manner interfere with, restrain, or coerce you in the exercise of the rights listed above.

WE WILL, to the extent we have not already done so, rescind and give no further effect to our unlawful rule announced orally and in writing between March and July of 2021, which restricted your access to nonwork areas of our facilities beyond fifteen minutes of the start and end of your shifts.

I can tell you right now that this notice was never posted anywhere "prominently," as Amazon was required to do. Instead, they sent a text out to workers, and they posted a notice in a tiny spot all the way in the corner on the first-floor break room. As you'll see in so many cases, I believe that companies like Amazon violate labor law because they know they'll get away with it. Even if they're slapped with a ULP complaint, they don't seem to care. We filed more than one hundred of those charges against them, but any financial penalties they get hit with are peanuts to them.

Unfortunately, too, they're unenforceable. Amazon or any other company can continue to contest penalties without anything happening. Still, some battles are worth the fight, and winning can make all the difference to your campaign. For us, that's what happened with the break rooms.

Four Simple Things: Community, Culture, Music, and Food

To a multitrillion-dollar company like Amazon, we were probably only seen as tiny irritants at first. Amazon is everywhere. It owns Zappos, Ring, Whole Foods, Twitch, and Prime Video. You can't live a regular day without running into an

Amazon Prime truck or hearing about one of their movies or a basketball game they're broadcasting. It's a company that permeates our lives. They can afford to spend millions on intimidation tactics, anti-union commercials, and social media ads, while we don't have the resources to do any of that. So how can David beat Goliath?

I believe we won our election with four simple concepts: **community and culture, plus music and food**. Whether or not your company is as big as Amazon, this is an approach that really brings about meaningful progress. Every day, when those six hundred to eight hundred workers got on and off the bus at work, we did our best to reach every single one of them. We had around thirty barbecues over an eleven-month period. We made bonfires at night: roasting marshmallows, playing the guitar, watching movies on the projector. We organized rallies and marched around the building and in the parking lot. We even brought politicians like Bernie Sanders and Alexandria Ocasio-Cortez to Staten Island, the reddest borough in New York, for the first time in history.

Our movement was successful, and attention-grabbing, because we purposefully created an intentional culture around labor organizing. Our goal was nothing short of making unions cool again for our specific community of workers, and to create an entirely new, fresh, and exciting culture around organizing.

We were the opposite of old-school. We were young. We were Black. And we did it our way. With our music. Our food. Our clothes. Our authentic style. In this way, **we created a space where all Amazon workers, from all races, cultures, and walks of life, could be themselves**, too. It was organizing that came from the bottom up, and not the top down.

I like to think that out there, at that now-legendary bus stop, what we really created was a place for rest and rejuvenation, a real **community**. Sometimes we would even pray together, hold hands, cry, or sing. We created a mental and physical space where everyone could unburden themselves. Chris put it well, I think, when he said our campaign was more than a labor union movement. It was a "spiritual experience" that was built from pure love and caring for one another.

I remember once when we held a fundraiser at the People's Forum in Manhattan. This was before we won the vote, and we all took turns speaking about why this movement was going to become something big and special. Jason Anthony, who was one of our core organizers from the start, was talking about how we were all like family. People were crying and feeling the truth of what he said.

I've been to plenty of old-school labor conferences. I've been to plenty of old-school labor parades. It's not a knock, but you see people there who've held office in their union for thirty or forty years. Those old-guard leaders have never been able to connect with young people, and that's a problem. Youth are the future of all unions. I'm thirty-five now, but I started off as a twenty-five-year-old just clocking in on a job like everybody else. I want to see other young people like me start their own unions, and to know that they, too, can carry the movement forward.

Ours was a movement led by people of color, but it was inclusive and made everyone feel welcome. Our leadership was Black, but we always had people from different backgrounds around us helping to move the group forward in some capacity. It never felt like anyone was excluded, or that they couldn't approach us.

Staten Island is the only red borough in New York City. There are Trump flags everywhere. But many of us made a conscious effort to avoid politics when we were talking to workers. Because if you feel that we all deserve to make thirty dollars an hour, then it doesn't matter which party you vote for or what color your skin is. If you agree that Jeff Bezos has made billions on the backs of workers who don't even get sick days, then we can get along with each other. That's how we brought people together. By building community through talking about the things that we all want for ourselves and for one another. We even conducted polls, asking workers questions and collecting data. "What things would you change about the company?" we asked. Their answers helped shape our demands, which we put right on the back of our T-shirts.

We were never about having a pinned-down, public relations–like approach. It was never just, "Hey. Here's a pamphlet. Have a good night." We spoke from the heart, and we were there, authentically and consistently, for people. We gave out free books, clothes, even marijuana. We helped people pay for Ubers in emergencies. Once, a worker with high blood pressure came out of the building. He needed to get to a hospital, but Amazon wouldn't pay for an Uber, which would cost around one hundred dollars. They told him to take the bus. We took care of it. We made sure he got to the hospital—and not on the bus.

There are workers who continue to call and text me in the middle of the night. They know that I'll go with them to HR and be their representative if something's wrong. My phone stays on. Chris likes to joke that I'll pick up for anybody. He's half-right: I will answer the phone for any worker. That's true. Because right now we still don't have a contract. And if somebody is going through something and they feel like they don't have any help from us, their first reaction is going to be disappointment. They'll say, "I thought the union was supposed to be there for me and they're not." I can't let that happen. So that's why I make myself as available as possible. I always give people my phone number (the real one) and tell them, "Any issue you're having, just text me."

When we were first starting out, sleeping at the bus stop, people were looking at us like we're crazy. They were like, "What are these guys doing out here? Passing out food and T-shirts?" But after a while it started to hit them. It got them thinking, "Wow, these people are really working hard for us." Sometimes I'd wake up and a worker would be right in my face, amazed. "Yo, you're still out here?!" they'd ask.

"Yeah, we're still here," I'd say. "We've been telling y'all that we're here for you."

They started to understand that I was out there on my day off. The only rest time I had was being dedicated to workers and to this movement.

When people ask how we created this amazing community of workers, one of the things we always say is that you need to think about what makes people feel comfortable and happy. I can think of two very important things that do both: music and food. Both were crucial to our movement.

Let's talk about **music** first. That's what kept us motivated and gave us confidence. It eased the tension. If you were walking toward the bus stop and you heard music, it opened the door to conversation. It helped people relax. Of course, traditional unions have music at their gatherings, but it doesn't necessarily speak to all workers effectively, and it's not always inclusive. One of the lessons we learned was how important it was to reflect the culture of the workforce at JFK8 in everything we did, including music. To do this, we set up a giant speaker that was connected to a generator and played a mix of new-school rap, R&B, reggae, and Afrobeats. Chris used to be a rapper when he was younger. He organized his own shows and used to see Drake and Kanye West at different venues. I know he even toured with Meek Mill for a little while. I was always into music as well, so this kind of vibe felt natural to us, and to many of the workers we wanted to reach. Music works wonders for all union movements, creating a welcoming, fun vibe and allowing people to get to know one another better. In our case, we added a special sauce by playing music that we knew resonated strongly with the mostly young Black and brown workers at JFK8.

In March 2021, a worker named Tristan Dutchin came to JFK8. He was a reggae musician, born and raised in Brooklyn with family roots from Guyana. Tristan played guitar and sang covers from artists like Bob Marley and Peter Tosh. I remember he used to come to the bus stop after his shift and make small talk with us. At first, he was shy and reserved, just like I used to be. I kind of saw him as a younger version of myself, so we really connected.

One day, he was leaving his shift, walking over to the bus stop. It was still his first month on the job, and I knew he was struggling. It was during Covid, and I was wearing my mask, holding a clipboard, and talking to a bunch of workers. At first, Tristan just sat down nearby and didn't say anything. Then, after a few minutes, he looked at me and just let it out, point-blank. He said, "Yo, bro. I been written up for some bullshit."

We talked about it for a while. He told me about how white supervisors at Amazon had made racist comments to him, and not for the first time. Back then, Tristan had dreadlocks, and I know he felt like he was being targeted by his supervisors for who he was and the way he looked. It seemed like he was always getting written up for something. He said one supervisor who wasn't even assigned to him made a point of going to his station just to tell him, "Don't steal nothing." The guy said it with a smile, like it was a joke. But Tristan knew it wasn't. He answered him in a very calm, respectful way, because that's how Tristan is. He just said, "No. I won't."

This wasn't the first time a worker had told me about experiencing racism on the job. The NLRB later ruled that Amazon broke the law when one of its union busters, Bradley Moss, pointed to a group of organizers and publicly called them "a bunch of thugs." Moss worked for the Burke Group, which specializes in "preventative labor relations," which would actually be a hilarious phrase if it weren't so sad.

Tristan's story wasn't the first I'd heard like this, and it wouldn't be the last. That was the moment when I asked him if he would sign an authorization card, and he didn't hesitate for a second. "I'm down," he said. From that point on, every time I saw him, Tristan kept me up-to-date on what was going on with him inside the building. He always asked a lot of questions about the union and was really engaged. Then, of course, when we had food, he would tear them doughnuts up.

I remember one day, early on, I gave him an assignment to help Chris set up the tent at JFK8. That was my way of helping to get him more involved. From that point on, Chris and Tristan really got to know each other better. Tristan told Chris that he was a musician, and Chris was like, "That's cool." He paused for a second and then added, "Do you have any cash right now?"

Honestly, Tristan was flat broke. He had like five dollars on him. That was one of those moments that Chris really showed himself as a true leader. He said, "I tell you what. You give me that five dollars, and I'll give you back one hundred dollars as your compensation for helping us out today." He knew Tristan needed that extra support and wanted to be there to give it to him. In May 2022, Tristan was fired. He was devastated. But we took care of him, encouraging him to provide entertainment for the group. As time went on, we watched Tristan become more and more confident as an organizer outside the facility and as a leader in his own right.

Later, Chris asked him to create an official ALU theme song, which he did. Tristan used a really cool nineties Jamaican dancehall playground rhythm and the song ended up becoming our anthem. We asked Tristan if he wanted to perform it publicly, which opened so many doors for him. We were proud to put him on our payroll in January 2023 as our first official ALU musician.

When the union leadership changed later, Tristan was taken off payroll, which wasn't a surprise to me. But he's still out there, to this day, performing his music at labor conferences across the country, speaking on panels, and helping to spread the word about the ALU. He's a very spiritual person who communicates a powerful message. "Keep going," he says. "Be a lion of strength. Be a lion of power. Sometimes the bad things have to happen first, before you can get to the good."

Like music, **food** is another powerful way of bringing people together. Everybody needs food, especially workers who are living check to check. I know there have been plenty of days when many of us couldn't even afford to buy lunch. Traditional unions know this, which is why they often have events and barbecues with hot dogs and burgers, especially on Labor Day. But we used food in a different way. It wasn't a special event; it was a regular, daily thing. We wanted people to know that when the ALU is out there, anyone can come and get a meal. We didn't have to rent out a hall for a special occasion, or set up a big event at a local park. And just like with the music, it was important to us to reflect the cultures of our membership in the food we offered. We made it our business to give out home-cooked food from around the world, everything from baked ziti and penne alla vodka, to African jollof rice and American soul food, like fried chicken, collard greens, and barbecue ribs. We made Spanish rice and Jamaican curry goat and jerk chicken. We did it all. It wasn't just, "Hey. Here's a sandwich or a hot dog." For us, it was about creating an environment with the kind of down-home comfort food that our members could relate to.

It sounds so simple, but it was so important. Free food makes people happy. We built trust and bonded as a community through our food. We knew that workers were much more likely to stop and have a conversation with us if they had something fresh, hot, and homemade to fill their stomachs.

This approach applies no matter where you work, but it was even more important at a place like Amazon, where the only food available inside JFK8 is processed foods and vending machines. There's no cafeteria. Amazon likes to take credit for "listening to workers." They say they brought in more food options because of the massive complaints about food from workers. And that's true. They do have vendors that come in now, but their prices are sky-high. Normally, if you go to any regular Popeye's, you might get a three-piece meal for nine dollars. At Amazon, when those vendors come in, the exact same meal will cost you sixteen dollars. Why is that? There's a huge markup, and I can only guess that Amazon is taking a cut, milking their own workers for extra profit.

This brings me to the final element that I think was key to our success, which is our **cultural authenticity**. You could call it our sense of style, but I think it goes much deeper than that. It's about showing up as you are and not letting anyone tell you that you need to change, or be something else, to succeed.

Chris wears big, chunky chains and rings and has tattoos everywhere, even on his neck. I don't even think he knows how many tattoos he has anymore. He probably lost count. I know they include a music scale and the names of his kids. Also, he wears durags, sweatpants, and dark sunglasses to meetings and media interviews. He shows up as he is, with his gold chains and gold grills.

When Bernie Sanders asked him to come testify about

Amazon's union-busting tactics and to help push for a Senate measure called Protecting the Right to Organize (PRO) Act, Chris wore his now-famous fire-engine-red jacket that says "Eat the Rich" and a New York Yankees baseball cap. He even wore this outfit to our meeting with President Joe Biden and Vice President Kamala Harris. Some people had negative things to say about that. But as I mentioned, we come as we are, with all our ALU merch and Jordans on full display, along with our jewelry and our tattoos. We don't change who we are for anyone, and our supporters wouldn't want us to. That is what authenticity looks like. (Also, Chris made it into *GQ* for his White House look, so it was all good.)

I'm a little more low-key in my appearance, personally, and I'm also not afraid to show up in a hoodie, jeans, and sneakers. I want to make the point that **what a "leader" looks like can be different for everyone**. We want kids and young people to understand that *this* is exactly what a leader can look like. Someone like us, and someone like them. That kind of authenticity resonates with younger workers, who especially like our logo and merchandise. As a matter of fact, they go crazy over it. A lot of unions don't really take a lot of pride in their branded hats and shirts, but we really do—especially because our stuff is different from what you might normally see a union selling.

There's our "Fight for $30" T-shirt, which refers to our goal of a thirty-dollar minimum wage. And the T-shirt with a full list of our demands on the back. It looks like this:

> **Higher pay, Health & safety, Abolish rate system, Better medical benefits, Retirement, Longer breaks, Better leave package, Job security, Weingarten rights, No forced overtime, Fair promotion policy**

Our clothes have a certain style that ended up becoming part of our persona as a union. The way I see it, you've got to really believe in what you're selling, whether it's a T-shirt or a philosophy. For us, everything went together. Everything with "ALU" on it reflected the lifestyle and culture of the four founders—and we succeeded by creating an inclusive community using music, food, and our own authentic culture and style.

But what happens if you're alone out there, in a company without close friends or a trusted team? How do you start? The first step is to figure out who you can trust. I know that can be hard. You've known people for only a few months sometimes, and in limited work-related settings. But before you invest your life and your livelihood in people, try to determine whether they're really someone you can count on to have your back. What's their history with friends and family? Are they loyal? Or do they have a sketchy record of betrayals?

Finding Potential Leaders

Nannette Plascencia is the lead organizer at the ONT8 warehouse in Moreno Valley, California. She's a veteran worker who's been at that facility since 2015. She's made amazing progress there, including positioning an organizer in every department for every shift. I know Chris has flown out to California at least eight times to support their efforts. That's a six-hour flight to LAX, plus an hour-and-forty-minute drive to Moreno Valley. He's gone repeatedly to stand in solidarity with workers there.

The problem is that Nannette has struggled to find other leaders to help her. She calls us and texts us a lot, asking for guidance. Oftentimes, she feels isolated and discouraged, and that understandably takes a serious toll on her ability to organize. The illegal manipulation and intimidation tactics used by the company have successfully scared a lot of people off. And unfortunately, in late 2022, ONT8 ended up withdrawing their petition for a union election. They needed more time to build and strengthen before taking that next step.

None of us can do this work alone. Once you've established a sense of trust with a few other workers, **you need to begin to identify more people around you who have leadership potential**. Finding them isn't always easy, but if you think about it, natural-born leaders usually have a way of standing out. You recognize them right away when you see them.

I can give you two examples.

There was a worker in my department named Genesis who was a natural leader. You could tell by watching her. At lunchtime she was always the center of attention among a huge group of Dominican friends who sat in what we call the "brick area" of the break room. She was like the glue that held the whole group together. They shared food and were always laughing with one another. If someone in the group had a birthday, they would bring cake and sing to them. But if Genesis happened to be out sick one day, the whole room was transformed. Some of the friends would just break off quietly and sit in other areas, just because she wasn't there. What was crazy was that as I watched Genesis, I saw that she didn't even recognize the power she had. I could see it, but I don't think she could.

You need to engage and educate natural-born leaders like Genesis first, because once you do that, they're going to relay the message to their friends in a far more powerful way than you ever could. When Genesis decided to support the union and sign an authorization card, I knew we had a massive positive force on our side. She now works in another area at JFK8, but she's still connected to all her old friends in my department, and I know they still respect her and listen to everything she says, including when it comes to the union.

Another example of a natural leader is Kim, who is Asian and Latino, which is important because my involvement with him is an example of how we reached out to, and interacted with, workers of all races and ethnic backgrounds. We were a Black-led movement, but contrary to what some would later say, we were inclusive of everyone. Kim has a great sense of humor and likes to make cracks at management. He'll always say things like, "Hey, I'm just here to get my money and go home." When you first meet him, you might not expect him to advocate for other workers because he doesn't seem all that serious. But there was an incident a few years ago that showed me he had real leadership potential.

It started as a problem with an old water fountain. A lot of workers used it to fill up jugs that are used to then pour water into a tape machine. Without water, the tape won't stick to the box, so the machine needs to stay full. Well, this old water fountain had mold everywhere. It was *bad*. And this was during Covid, which didn't help the situation since some people were even using it to drink from.

Kim was really frustrated. He'd say, "Look at all this mold! People are putting their mouths on it. It's disgusting!" He went to management repeatedly to tell them about it, but they never responded. That's when Kim surprised me and started going up to other workers.

"Hey!" he'd yell to them. "We need to do something about this!" Most of the people he talked to were scared to speak out. They didn't want to risk getting written up or fired. But Kim took the issue all the way to the general manager. He simply wouldn't stop. He kept saying, "We need some new water fountains!"

Finally, he got exactly what he asked for. Amazon replaced the old fountains with the modern, motion-sensor water fountains that most workplaces have now.

Even though he never seemed like someone who wanted

to get involved in organizing, I saw how Kim showed real leadership skills, which allowed him to win that battle. He's someone I've kind of kept my eye on over the years, keeping him updated on union activities in the hope that he might develop as even more of a leader one day. This is how you organize from within. Not every person has to be on the front line, and Kim is still involved with the union even if he's not there for every action. You have to cultivate any worker who has this kind of leadership potential, one by one, in the hope that they might become even more visible and active in your movement. His example reminds me that everyone has their own personal atomic moment. For Kim, that moment was the water fountains.

Trust Your Instincts

One of the most important things you can do when starting your campaign sounds simple but is also the most difficult: **trust yourself**. We can talk about the importance of trusting your instincts going all the way back to when Chris and I first decided to launch our campaign, during that long drive home from Bessemer, Alabama. We were fired up and ready to get started. We thought, "Let's strike while the iron is hot!" We had seen and learned more about what to do, and what not to do, and felt the timing was right to bring those lessons to JFK8.

But some of our supporters hesitated. Especially the

salts. They were the mostly white college student transplants who joined our movement from the outside, and many of them were afraid that we weren't ready. Some thought we all needed to study more, and that we should work with experts like the late Jane McAlevey, a highly respected union activist and scholar, to understand more about the unionizing process before beginning. The salts were in touch with McAlevey, who was advising us informally, sharing videos about how to communicate effectively with other workers. One of the salts even arranged for us to take some online training courses with her to learn more about building up a campaign.

It wasn't like doing more research and studying was a bad idea, exactly. Chris and I signed up for the classes, just to make everyone feel better. But in the end, neither of us ever got a chance to take those courses. We had other priorities and ultimately felt that the moment was right for action, not talk. And not studying. If you think about it, no one had ever done what we were doing at the company we were doing it at—and so no one could really tell us exactly how to do it.

You can't always wait until others are ready. Or until they think you're ready. Trust yourself. And when you're ready, you'll know.

4.

The Biggest Challenges

How to Have Difficult Conversations

At its core, organizing is about having tough conversations. You need to have them all day, every day, with workers who may be exhausted, disinterested, skeptical, hostile, or all of the above. They probably work ten to twelve hours. Some have families to take care of, too. Some don't want to hear about *anything*. So you need to make sure that when you approach them, you come correct. Explain yourself clearly. Be confident in what you're saying. Because if you don't believe what you're saying, those employees are going to tune you out right away. In my organizing journey, I've learned how important it is to tap into your own emotional intelligence to determine exactly which direction to take a conversation in and how to keep it going.

I don't go by any kind of script. I've always operated by instinct, which has taught me so much about trusting my own people skills. **Organizing is about knowing how to read people and relate to them.** If there's a worker I've never talked to a day in my life, I'm not going to go up to them cold and start talking about organizing. I'm going to approach them thoughtfully and get a sense of where they are. Start with a basic conversation: what's their name, how long they've been with the company, what department they're in. Baby steps.

It is also true, though, that some organizers have a totally different style. They come on strong, jumping right in:

"Here's what a union does, and this is why you need to join. Sign here!" That might work for some, but I believe it's more effective when an organizer builds a personal relationship with people. I don't believe in bringing forceful energy to my conversations. You can't force a New Yorker to do nothing, anyway. That's number one. So the wording you choose means everything.

To begin, I want to **get to know them and how they're navigating the workplace**. Are they having arguments with management? Do they come to work frustrated? Is there anything they'd like to change? If they're having issues with commuting, I let them know that we're working on getting a shuttle for people, so they don't have to take the bus to the ferry. I cater to their needs, talk about the things that relate to them directly. What are their goals? Even their hobbies. What are they into?

Depending on their responses, I might share a little bit about my own work story at that point: how long I've been with the company, and why I decided to form a union. I'll try to relate to their pain and share similar experiences in the hope of building a bond.

And then I may just leave it at that. Because I know I'll see them again, so I let it develop in a gradual way. **Successful organizing is about creating genuine bonds based on shared concerns.** It's not about forcing yourself and your opinion on people. It is about listening and about meeting people where they are.

If the person is really interested in what I'm saying and

fully engaged, I'll keep going. But if it's not happening today, that's fine. I let 'em go. Because I remember faces. And I know workers at the bus stop are going to be there the next day and the day after that. I can wait it out. Next time I see them, I can go back and ask them how the day was and try again.

I'm a big believer in energy. People can feel it. Animals, too. Jordan's cat, Jinx, is funny. He doesn't seem to like anyone except me. Every time I'm on the couch he jumps up right beside me. He doesn't even do that to Jordan. For whatever reason, I guess he likes my energy.

My Three (Actually, Four) Toughest Kinds of Workers

If I were to describe the most challenging types of workers, I would put them into three categories: immigrants, recent high school or college graduates, and the actively anti-union worker.

By far, the most difficult demographic to reach, for me, has been undocumented immigrants. Some might not have any kind of papers. Amazon employs undocumented workers, and in early 2025 we even had ICE raids at JFK8. These workers are understandably terrified. Companies tell workers that their immigration status or work permits will be affected if they join a union. They know that if they slip up even a little, they can be deported. There's no way they're going to risk standing out or making waves. The first thing you want to do is simply gain these workers' trust. See if you can have a conversation about their concerns. The threat of an ICE raid is real. Let them know that someone from the union can stand with them if needed. Even if they don't show public support by signing an authorization card or wearing union merchandise, one of these workers may be helping behind the scenes, which is still a win.

Another group that I find challenging are the workers that are fresh out of high school or college. They're skeptical and seem to be kind of removed from what their coworkers are going through. To me, it sometimes seems like the only thing they're focused on is whatever's going on inside their phone. Many of them are still living at home and not worried about making a living wage, paying bills, or earning a pension. They're working so they can buy new sneakers or have pocket money. That's a very different scenario from someone who's trying to support a family. I've also noticed that this type of worker often doesn't have a good understanding of what a union is about. I'll sit with them and try to break down the history. It might just start with a head nod at the bus stop. Later, maybe I'll also ask them if they have a parent that was in a union, which can sometimes help to break the ice. In those cases, I try hard to connect and to be up to speed with how they move in the world. A lot of these young workers care about clothes and branding, which is another reason our sense of style and our merchandise was so successful. It really spoke to them.

The third type is the hardcore anti-union worker. Of all the stubborn people I've encountered while organizing for the ALU, these are some of the toughest. At first, anti-union workers may not seem like they're worth the effort. But the truth is, they're a key part of any union drive. If you're able to flip an anti-union person, especially the loudest and most outspoken one, then you're really getting somewhere. Because that loud, outspoken anti-union person is also a leader. They have influence over other people. So one important goal is to try to get to know people in their circle of friends. Not all of their friends will be anti-union. Sometimes you can recruit one or two of them to help educate this more combative worker so that they'll at least listen to another perspective.

I've seen that some dollar store workers in the South are trying a completely different approach. They don't use the word "union" at all. Instead, groups like Step Up Louisiana are talking to workers about how they can make changes without even becoming a union to avoid the negative associations some right-to-work states have with that term.

Why are some people so anti-union? They might have been in unions in the past and felt disappointed, like the organization didn't serve them. I've heard a lot of stories that start with, "Oh, I got fired and the union didn't protect me." But in some of those cases, as the person keeps talking, I discover that they got fired because of their own mistakes. Let's be clear about one thing: The union is there to protect people from *unlawful and retaliatory* firing. Just because you're in a union doesn't mean you can get away with wrongdoing and breaking rules.

Another common myth anti-union workers will throw out is: "The union will take your money, but they don't do nothing for you." But all they need to do is look at me to know that's not true. I'm out here 24-7 helping workers. Day and night. Even before we have a contract. Again, consistency is key. I always explain that this is a brand-new, worker-led, grassroots union, not like what they may have experienced before, or what their parents may have experienced in a traditional union with a huge bureaucracy and leadership that's out of touch with its members.

Most importantly, I try to show them that I'm here for them anytime—to help with any problems they may be having on the job, or just to listen to their concerns. Amazon is big on saying workers should be able to "speak for themselves." The company drills it into them that the union is a "third party." How does that make sense when it's a collective of us, speaking for ourselves, together? The voice of one person alone can only go so far with a company like Amazon. Again, just look at my example. I was outspoken and fought for what I deserved, but that didn't get me anywhere. A union can fight for the greater good of workers, in a powerful and legal way.

There's also a fourth category of workers, which is a little harder to identify. These are people who, deep down, just don't feel like they really deserve thirty dollars an hour or whatever benefits the union wants to ensure. Call it low self-esteem or lack of confidence. They may be soft-spoken or not trying to call attention to themselves. Whatever the reason, they're managing to get by with the bare minimum and feel that's the best they can do. In those cases, you need to help that person to look inside and understand why they feel this way. Sometimes our self-esteem has been hit so hard that we don't even think we're worth the struggle. It may sound crazy, but some people truly feel like they don't deserve more in life. Getting to them and helping them to reflect on that is hard, but we need to try. Have direct conversations with them and encourage them to express concerns. What specific issues or problems are they having on the job? Show consistency. Be available to them for whatever they may need, whenever they may need it. If they need to go to HR or are being disciplined, they probably will be grateful for your support in facing that conflict.

The Importance of Patience and Timing

Even if somebody doesn't agree with the union at first, it is crucial to **keep talking to and engaging with them**. Because ultimately, everyone wants a raise. Everyone wants job security. Everyone wants a better quality of life and a safe workplace. One of our most basic demands at Amazon is for two thirty-minute breaks and an hour-long lunch. Everyone wants that.

There is a woman I worked with, Michelle, whose story

shows the importance of staying engaged until the timing is right. When I first approached her in July 2021, we were just starting to get authorization cards signed and I didn't really know her at all. I started by asking, "How long have you been with the company?" She said she'd been there for three years, which was a good sign. It meant she had already been through and seen a lot. I felt confident asking if she wanted to sign the authorization card.

"Yeah," she said. "You know, I think we need some change at JFK8."

That was the perfect response right there. She signed the card, and I left it at that, because the fact that she signed was already a huge step. I knew I could go into more details later. However, I did get her Facebook handle, because she struck me as a cool person. I thought to myself, "Let me just see what her life is like outside of Amazon."

That's where things got interesting. When I started following her on Facebook, I noticed that she had some older posts about unions from back in the thirties, forties, and fifties. I figured, "Okay, there's some general interest here." Later, when we were back on the same shift, I asked, "How do you feel about the ALU? Do you think we're going to make some good changes?" She was a soft-spoken person. "Yeah," she said. "I do."

I told her about the barbecues we were hosting and invited her to come out and get some food. But she never came. Weeks went by, and then months. During that time, I would still ask, "Hey, you want to come to the barbecue today?"

Because we were constantly having barbecues. Sometimes she'd say she'd come, but then she never did. Still, I continued to engage with her. I was never going to say, "Hey, why didn't you come to the barbecue?" It was all good. I knew this was a long game.

Fast-forward to the captive audience meetings, where workers are required to go and listen to anti-labor speeches, and basically be brainwashed by the union-busting consultants the company spends millions of dollars on. Basically, **these are designed to force workers to listen to the company's position**, which is that unions are inherently damaging and destructive. Since there's usually no other voice in the room, and since attendance is mandatory, it's literally like workers are being held "captive" and forced to ingest propaganda without ever hearing the other side.

Amazon held captive audience meetings every day, and I often saw Michelle there. At these meetings, which I'll talk about later in more detail, I always spoke out, offering facts about unions and calling out the truth about how these meetings are designed to convince workers to vote no.

One day, as I went back and forth with the consultants, I noticed that Michelle spoke up in favor of the union, too. "Okay, now we're getting somewhere," I thought. "She's talking now, expressing her feelings." When the meeting was over, I pulled up beside her and said, "Can you believe that?" That's when she went off. "I cannot believe what they're doing! This is so wrong!" This was the moment I was waiting for. We were walking and talking, and after a few minutes I said, "Look, I know you have an interest in unions. I want to really get you on board and get you organizing with us."

The timing was right. She said yes without any hesitation. The next day, she came to the break room and passed out union pamphlets with us. She started wearing our T-shirts, coming to our weekly Zoom meetings, and dedicating her time to the ALU. Eventually, she became a secretary on our executive board. Her example shows the importance of continuing to stay in contact with workers, waiting for your moment, and taking the time to really get to know them. We would later lose Michelle's support, unfortunately. But that's a longer story, and one that I'll also talk about later.

It's important to realize that even when people may not seem to be interested, the information you're giving them stays in the back of their head. The moment they come back to you is often the moment they get their first write-up or confront any kind of official work trouble. At Amazon, getting a write-up is the turning point for a lot of workers because they're being written up for things that don't make sense to them and things that are just plain unfair. At that moment, people are scared. They need this job and don't understand what's happening. Getting a write-up is like the beginning of the end at Amazon. At that point, the system is designed to eliminate you. After you start getting write-ups, it's only a matter of time before you're out of there.

Here's how it works at Amazon: One write-up is supposed to last thirty days. If you mess up again within thirty days, then comes a second write-up, which you're very likely to get because managers specifically target and monitor workers who've already gotten their first write-up. Even if the first write-up does go away in thirty days, that doesn't mean it really went away. Because if you get six write-ups within a year, you're automatically terminated. Here's the crazy part: Sometimes workers won't even know they've gotten write-ups. Their manager won't tell them. They'll just put it into the system.

The company policy says that managers are supposed to engage with workers. There's something called a "seek to understand," where managers ask if there's a good reason behind the write-up. Was there a barrier that got in their way? Managers need to give workers an opportunity to express their side. But they don't always follow these rules. So now, you may have a worker who's gotten several write-ups and didn't know about any of them. They get called down to HR out of the blue and are told, "This is your last day. You're being terminated."

At that moment, I need to be there for that worker doing whatever I can, whether it's advocating on their behalf with HR or helping them to file a ULP complaint. Looking back, I can remember so many times where I've just said to myself, "Okay, *now* this person really needs me." **You need to recognize those instances when company policy becomes harmful, and use them to help workers understand what the union is all about.**

The fall of 2022 was a key moment for a lot of workers at JFK8. That's when the time for action was suddenly right for us. On October 3 of that year, at about 4:00 p.m., a cardboard compactor caught on fire inside the building. It wasn't a small fire, either. Even after the flames were put out, there was still a lot of smoke in the air. People were coughing and there were obvious safety issues. The daytime workers, who had been evacuated almost at the end of their shift, were sent home with pay. I knew about this because the day-shift workers had sent me a video of the fire, which we immediately put up on TikTok. It got more than half a million views.

But what made the situation worse was that supervisors didn't seem to have any idea how to manage people as this was taking place. There were visually impaired workers on the day shift, for example, who had to be led outside by other workers because the managers and supervisors weren't paying any attention.

At the same time, the night-shift workers had no idea that anything was even happening. They were told to clock in and go wait in the main break room. I remember seeing maybe four hundred people in there with no clue about what was going on. The room looked like it was even over capacity.

The union had been voted in just six months earlier, in April 2022, and even though Amazon had refused to recognize us, I knew that since I was vice president, people were depending on me to represent workers' rights. I'm proud to say that I led an effort to keep them safe that day inside the building. I made sure to show them all the video and to fill them in on what was happening, while our team was simultaneously advocating for them to be sent home with pay.

Eventually, our demands ended up evolving into a kind of sit-in protest, right there in the break room, which then led to a march to the main office. It was an actual rally right there inside JFK8. In the end, about two dozen workers from the night shift were suspended with pay for refusing to work. I was suspended too, with pay, along with everyone else. But what Amazon didn't realize (again) was that suspending us had the opposite effect than they intended. Union support went through the roof! **People saw that the union was fighting hard for them, regardless of the consequences.**

This led Amazon to retaliate with a new policy. I had been working the day shift when the fire broke out, but I stayed after work to advocate for night-shift workers. Because of this, I believe that Amazon decided to impose a new rule saying that workers whose shifts were over couldn't stay in the building for more than fifteen minutes after their shift ended. This was just one of their many counterattacks against us. As you'll see in the next section, Amazon spent nearly $13 million on union busting in 2024 alone. You have to wonder what would happen if they spent even a fraction of this on making the workplace safer and fairer. Wouldn't that kind of investment be better for everyone, including them?

Popular Counterattacks Used by Companies

In April 2025, Bloomberg reported that a group of sixty-eight Amazon investors signed a letter raising concerns about Amazon's decision to shut down all seven of its warehouses in Quebec, which resulted in the termination of thousands of workers there who had been engaged in unionizing and collective bargaining negotiations. "We are surprised," the letter said, that "the company is making a strategic business decision to close its operations so suddenly and so soon after expanding operations and investment in Quebec."

Shutting down completely was a radical counterattack, but there are also many other strategies used by companies to crush labor movements. In some cases, key individuals will be disciplined or fired. A classic example of this is the case of the Memphis Seven, the seven Starbucks employees who were illegally fired from a store in Tennessee after they organized a union. The NLRB ruled that the firings were retaliatory, and a federal judge ordered Starbucks to reinstate the employees.

There are plenty of other tactics that may be used as well. For example, another tactic might be to impose one-on-one meetings with individual workers and management, sometimes even in a worker's own home. Companies will also offer promotions or raises as a way to cultivate "backdoor" relationships with outlier workers who may be on the fence about joining a union. In this way, management tries to chip away at the unity of the collective.

How can workers combat these attacks? It all comes down to education and information. The goal is to enlighten but in a way that is always careful to reflect solidarity and to avoid judgment. It's important to ask questions, like: Why is management offering you this promotion right now? Why are they interested in meeting with you one-on-one at this moment when there's a union campaign? And why did it take a union coming in for them to give you these opportunities for upward mobility?

What makes these counterattacks so effective is that they aren't confined to a single event. Companies use a wide variety of tactics. In fact, **union-busting tactics and philosophies are woven into the very fabric of corporate culture**. Once the union campaign goes live, these tactics become part of everything you see and do on the job. They're not the same at every workplace, but there are common threads. Often, workers will find anti-union language and training strategies in company handbooks, on bathroom walls, and in orientation meetings and introductions. Some will receive text messages and emails.

At Amazon, one of the things they warn new workers about is people talking in groups. "If you see a group of workers talking," the company says, "go tell a manager." It doesn't matter what the conversation might be about. When workers gather, Amazon even has a word for it. They call it "conjuring," and it's always a bad thing from the company's perspective.

This kind of policy ensures that other workers become eyes and ears for management. They're surveilling you, contributing to union busting. Many workplaces require new employees to watch training videos that talk about looking out for the "warning signs" of potential organizing, like someone taking an "unusual interest in policies and benefits." Just think about that for a minute. If a worker is interested in learning about company policies and benefits, why is that automatically seen as a threat? Amazon isn't the only company that creates and utilizes these kinds of videos. Places like Home Depot, Target, and many other companies employ the exact same training techniques and strategies.

Another rule that's woven into the training culture at many companies is that they tell workers not to give out their names or phone numbers to anyone, implying that fellow workers are going to harm them by making contact. There are even "union words" for managers to watch out for, like "living wage" and "grievance." These words are painted as being dangerous.

Workers at LDJ5, which is a smaller Staten Island warehouse across the street from us, voted 618 to 380 against joining the ALU. That was like a punch to the gut. Amazon used its counterattacks well in that building. Those fifteen hundred workers were persuaded by everything the company told them. They let the union busting get to them and didn't have the strength in numbers to fight it. We can learn from those counterattacks.

At LDJ5, union busters passed out fliers and put messages on vending machines that said, "THE ALU IS TRYING TO INSULT YOUR INTELLIGENCE." They were constantly pushing this idea that it was better to have a "direct" relationship with the company. Their angle was, "You don't need a union to fight your battles for you. You're smart enough to think for yourself and to handle any issues on your own." They said union officers could "put you on trial and fine or expel you." Crazy stuff. Most of the workers there are part-time. They're not making enough money whatsoever and can't afford to lose that job. Amazon made them promises, saying if they voted no to the union, they would get this or that reward. But of course, that never happened.

We had a barbecue later, after the vote, to try to bring everyone together. Some of the LDJ5 folks told us that they regretted voting no and wanted the chance to vote again. But now they need to take the time to really build support and be fully prepared before trying again. If they aren't, having two losses in the same building will be devastating for morale.

Countering these messages and tactics is challenging because most of us don't have the resources to create fancy training videos and commercials. So we need to do what we can to counter this propaganda with our own tools, outreach, and social media platforms.

When we first started our campaign, we had no playbook. As Chris put it, we were just "week to week playing chess with Amazon." There was always something new to deal with: another false rumor, another union-busting tactic. Organizers starting out should know right out of the gate that there's nothing easy about organizing. Companies will retaliate against you in ways both big and small. Being prepared for their reactions and knowing how to navigate them are key.

For me, a lot of the immediate, personal reactions I faced were cold stares and side conversations from managers and supervisors. I'd be at my station working and they would be huddled up together, staring at me. I'd look over and they'd look away. It was ridiculous. Childish. From the very beginning, I came to work wearing my Congress of Essential Workers T-shirt. Managers would point at me and then point at the shirt. All of that was supposed to intimidate me. But I knew I just needed to keep doing my job, and doing it well, so that I could continue to be the voice of associates inside the building.

But sometimes the retaliation can be bolder.

On April 29, 2021, just nine days after we'd started getting authorization cards signed for the ALU, I was told by my manager that I needed to get up on a narrow catwalk on the third floor to do jam clearing. It wasn't a solid platform, and it wasn't safe. Also, it was in a strange location, kind of in the back, away from everybody. I asked her, "Okay, what's the purpose of this assignment? And why am I being separated from everyone else?" No one could give me any kind of explanation that made sense. Clearly, the goal was to isolate me. So, after a while, I took matters into my own hands. I said, "Okay. I know why you're doing it. Just take me off and put me back on the floor." And they did. That little stunt didn't even last more than a couple of hours.

Captive Audience Meetings

By far, one of the most brutal and effective counterattacks from companies is captive audience meetings, as mentioned earlier. These are a tried-and-true union-busting tactic. They're powerful, and they're pervasive.

As soon as we submitted our authorization cards in October 2021, when Amazon realized that our movement was gaining traction and that the union was really happening, they immediately started holding captive audience meetings. In the time leading up to the vote, there were captive audience meetings every single day. In fact, every fifteen minutes, Amazon sent messages to different departments instructing them to attend one of these meetings. They had to convince workers to vote no, and these meetings were their main forum for getting it done. Jodi Kantor of *The New York Times* reported that Amazon spent $4.3 million that year alone on anti-union consultants. They weren't alone. A 2019 Economic Policy Institute report found that, overall, U.S. companies spend a total of about $340 million a year on union-busting consultants.

In these meetings, they'll tell you that union organizers are "outsiders" and that workers should keep a "direct" relationship with management for their own protection. This makes no sense. We were workers, just like everyone else, organizing from the inside. Any labor activists we may have had on the outside and working with us in solidarity didn't change that. The company will also try to scare workers by saying they can lose pay and benefits if they unionize. Also not true. It's illegal for a company to punish workers by taking away pay or benefits. When collective bargaining begins, you start with what you already have and gain more. Any changes negotiated can only be approved by the workers.

These meetings are basically full of propaganda. Company videos and paid union busters come in saying that we're all "one team" working together. They talk about how we've come so far and are "celebrating our inclusivity and diversity." They talk about improvements they've made thanks to "open communication" and a "direct" relationship with workers. (That's a joke. Like the time when they required us to buy "safety shoes" that no one asked for or wanted and gave us coupons from Zappos, an Amazon-owned company, to do so.)

Some companies, like Trader Joe's, do one-on-one meetings instead, where they can harass employees individually. But no matter how different companies do it, the goal is always the same. Companies lie in these meetings, and they manipulate, using every argument they can think of to get workers to vote no. The information they feed you is designed to drain your energy and deter you from even talking about unions.

I have actual audio from one of these meetings, where a supervisor tells workers that the union wants to "shut down Amazon." What? How does that even make sense? Again, they will lie, manipulate, and say anything to stoke fear. But one thing that we did differently at JFK8 was we made it our business **to speak out consistently at every meeting we could**.

For example, one of Amazon's main arguments is that workers should be allowed to speak for themselves, and to have a "direct relationship" with the company. They say that we should continue working with management as one team. I interrupted right there. "This is bullshit," I said. Just like that. "How are we working as one team if we're being ignored? How are we 'one team' when all Amazon cares about is profit?" When they tried to silence me, I said, "Nah. Hold up. This is nothing but a union-bashing session."

My speaking up in that forum really resonated because it got other workers involved, and it caught Amazon by surprise. I think they assumed they were going to go in there and say whatever they wanted about unions, and it would be unchallenged. They thought workers were going to soak up their propaganda.

Every meeting, consultants would say, "ALU's a third

party." I'd stop them and ask, "How are we a third party? I'm picking. I'm packing. I'm stowing. I'm on my feet for ten hours. I have a blue badge. I work overtime. How am I a third party?" In fact, the consultants who hold these meetings are the *real* third party. They're senior management leaders who are flown in from other states and put up at the Hilton down the street. They're driving BMWs, walking around with suits and ties, and telling crowds of workers not to fight for thirty dollars an hour. How can *they* be valid spokespeople for workers? They have no credibility. They don't even try to hide what they're doing. Honestly, after a while, the hypocrisy and endless presentations start to wear you down.

But organizing from the inside means that at least I'm there. I can speak up and say, "No. We're not going to allow these lies to be told. We're going to speak the truth. We're going to challenge this." When I started offering facts about unions, the consultants had nothing to say in rebuttal. I remember the first time I did it, they had to call in another consultant, who wasn't even at the meeting. He came in suddenly to come shut the whole thing down early because they were looking bad and didn't have anything to say. Later, when it was time for managers to gather their workers for the forced meetings downstairs, I felt that they deliberately skipped over me. Not just me. Lots of other organizers, too.

All of this proves that we were having an impact, and it brings me back to my earlier point about organizing from the inside. **You *must* have someone in the room who can**

stand up and challenge the lies that are being told. Otherwise, workers who know nothing about unions will simply digest that information as is.

What happens on the inside can be a mind-blowing experience. I saw up close how all those captive audience meetings were supposed to crush us day after day. Instead, we flipped the narrative by challenging the brainwashing. We used the meetings to gather even more support, and in the end, they ended up playing a huge part in our success.

More Lessons Learned: North Carolina

I'm not going to lie. We've had some brutal losses. In many cases, in other locations, Amazon's counterattacks have worked. We expected that. Remember, this is David going up against Goliath. You're not going to win every time. But there are some situations where you can see clearly what went wrong, mistakes that could have been prevented and warning signs that should have been noticed before the vote. In these cases, we need to study our playbook closely, to better understand what to do and what not to do next time.

Of all the Amazon facilities that tried to unionize after us, workers at the RDU1 fulfillment center near Raleigh, North Carolina, came the closest. They called themselves Carolina Amazonians United for Solidarity and Empowerment, or CAUSE. They put in a lot of work and did a lot of things right. In fact, they watched us very closely and followed our blueprint 100 percent. Out of all the different campaigns around the country, they were the ones who copied our formula best.

Their situation was a lot like ours, too. They had about forty-five hundred workers, which is close to what we have at JFK8. Both are fulfillment centers. Their president and vice president are Black, like it was with me and Chris. Reverend Ryan Brown, who is also a Baptist pastor, and Mary Hill, who they call "Ma Mary," were the leaders there. They organized inside the facility and outside. They were active on social media. And they hosted lots of community events. They weren't barbecues like ours, and they weren't out there all the time, but they were able to create a sense of coalition and togetherness.

I like the way Mary Hill describes the beginning of the movement, which, like us, became strong during Covid. They saw the ambulances coming to the building every day, she says. Sometimes they came two and three times a day. Workers there knew something was wrong with the way Amazon was handling the pandemic. Rev. Ryan went home and prayed about it. And as he did, he got one word: organize. What's funny about the story is that, at the time, he really didn't know what the message meant. "Organize what?" he wondered.

Back at work he had identified four people he wanted to talk to about it. But something strange happened each time he approached one of them. Again, he heard from God. "No. Not that one," he was told. "Talk to *her*." The "her" was Ma Mary, an Amazon worker and longtime community activist. Ryan didn't really like this idea. He said, "I'm not going to go talk to that mean Black lady." At least that's how Mary tells the story. As she puts it, some people do think she's blunt.

But Ryan did eventually talk to her. Mary explained to him that they needed a good name to start a campaign. Something that would stick. She came up with CAUSE. Mary was older than many of the workers and had already had a lifetime of work experience. In the 1970s, she worked at Mesa Fiberglass, a fabrication plant in Denver, Colorado, where workers had a union. She was already familiar with what it meant to have those benefits and advantages.

The organizing efforts of CAUSE worked well, and they started really gaining traction. One of their mottos was, "I am not a robot." It was printed on placards at every rally and every event, and it captured the mood and the feeling that Amazon didn't care about workers as human beings.

But it was always going to be a tough fight organizing in North Carolina. First, because they're a right-to-work state where union membership is among the lowest in the entire country. Nationally, around 10 percent of workers belong to unions, but in North Carolina, only about 2.4 percent of the population are union members. So CAUSE made history by even having a vote.

But Amazon pulled out all its usual counterattacks, and the campaign was overwhelmed. In December 2024, just a few weeks before the election, Amazon fired Rev. Ryan, too, which didn't help. CAUSE lost the vote by a landslide: 2,447 to 829.

What went wrong? The answer to that question is, from my point of view, painfully obvious. When you announce that you're going to have an election, here's how it's supposed to go: Workers recommend a date to the NLRB. The company is then supposed to either agree or counter with a different date. In the case of the ALU, Amazon tried to make us have the election within a month, but there was no way we were going to do that, so we fought it.

We filed for an election in December, and the vote took place between March 25 and 30. That meant we had a full three months to organize. **This time is vital, because in a way you're starting a whole new campaign now, one that begins after the authorization cards are in.** That time played a huge part in us being able to make sure that we had enough people to vote yes.

In North Carolina, it didn't play out that way. Instead of fighting for a date that worked for them, they allowed Amazon to set the date for *four weeks* from the time the vote was announced. It's shocking to me that they had an AFL-CIO union lawyer who seemed to agree to this. Their lawyers were paid a retainer fee, but the truth is, they didn't have any skin in the game. They weren't as invested as you would hope a legal team would be. So CAUSE relied on this legal advice that **the election should be held as soon as possible, which was a huge mistake**. I understand that they're in the process of looking for new legal representation right now.

They jumped the gun, as Mary puts it. But she also points out that the local NLRB office in Winston-Salem seemed to have a certain bias in their control of the process. They said the vote had to be according to their calendar and wouldn't budge, either. Mary says she watched the interactions between the NLRB representative and one of the main union busters hired by Amazon, and their relationship seemed a little too cozy.

We met with CAUSE several times over the years, giving feedback and offering advice. Throughout the campaign they had asked us for ideas, but strangely, when it came to the decision on when to hold the election, they did their own thing. We could have told them that agreeing to such a short time frame was a death knell for their campaign. Why didn't they communicate with us on such an important question? I have my theories. The two founders of CAUSE are Black, but everyone around them is white. Again, when we were there, we got some pushback from these other organizers about coming from the North, telling them how to do things.

"In the South, you still have a lot of people with that Jim Crow attitude," Mary later told me. Some workers are still a product of that environment. The feeling we got from some white organizers, and what they were communicating to us, was that they knew better how to talk to people in the South than we did. Chris and I both felt that at some point they poisoned the water. They decided they didn't feel like asking Black men from New York for advice about how they should be organizing in North Carolina.

The other huge mistake they made was **allowing the election to be held *inside* the warehouse**. Why would you do that? Workers are already intimidated. They already feel surveilled. Why would you give Amazon the upper hand by allowing them to control the setting? Mary points out that, again, local NLRB representatives made this decision along with Amazon. They said they didn't want to be out in the cold. Again, we would have told them this was a mistake. If only they had asked.

We've talked a lot about creating community and the importance of having union leadership that reflects all the different ethnicities and cultures of workers. In the state of North Carolina and at this Amazon facility, they have workers from Creole and Cajun backgrounds, as well as Spanish- and Arabic-speaking immigrants. The organizers there had nobody in place to speak to those workers, or to relate to them culturally and emotionally. "We didn't think about any of that," Mary later told me. That gap meant that Amazon could jump right in with its union-busting message. They told workers they would get deported if they voted yes, and it worked.

Now it's up to Ma Mary and Rev. Ryan and the others to regroup and figure out how to come back from a failed campaign. Rev. Ryan tells me they're in the process of "rediscovery, rethinking, and restructuring." I know for a fact that this is true and am absolutely sure of one thing: when they emerge again, CAUSE is going to be more powerful than ever.

5.

Playing the Long Game

To Engage (or Not to Engage) Celebrity Politicians

Ours was one of the most important union campaigns in modern history. Yet some of the people you might think would have supported us did not. The celebrity politicians that we expected to show up stayed radio silent until we won the election. That's when everybody jumped on the bandwagon. Seeing that happen was a huge disappointment, and one we didn't expect.

In the beginning of our campaign, we were excited about reaching out to some key legislators, especially those who support social justice and labor movements, and getting their help rallying workers before the vote. Chris and I took the train to Washington, DC, for National Moral Monday, which was a protest organized by Rev. William J. Barber II and Rev. Jesse Jackson during Covid as part of the Poor People's Campaign. Some legislators were at the U.S. Capitol, protesting the end of the eviction moratorium by sleeping outside on the steps. We decided to go try to meet with Representative Cori Bush, who started that movement. It went well. We got to sit with Representative Bush and talk for a while. We took a picture with her, and she said she would get in touch.

Unfortunately, she never did.

We also met with Representative Alexandria Ocasio-Cortez and got a picture with her, too. She was another figure who didn't get back to us until we'd already won the vote. That was when she posted three biceps emoji on Twitter in response to the victory. Podcaster Krystal Ball called her out, reminding her that ALU organizers had been disappointed by her lack of support throughout the campaign, and pointing out that "these are your constituents." That's when AOC made another huge mistake. She tweeted back that JFK8 "isn't in my district and maybe you should look at a map before claiming so." That was just another slap in the face. In fact, her tweet bothered me so much that I also had to call her out publicly when I was asked about it in an interview.

Ocasio-Cortez represents District 14, which covers parts of the Bronx and Queens, and includes City Island, Van Nest, Morris Park, Astoria, Jackson Heights, Woodside, and lots of other neighborhoods with Puerto Rican, Mexican, Ecuadorian, Indian, and Dominican New Yorkers. Thousands of people in her district commute to work at Amazon. Workers come from all five boroughs, plus New Jersey. It was laughable for her to even say that. My response got a lot of attention. Later, she had to come out and apologize for that tweet. It wasn't her best moment, and she knew it.

More than anyone else, however, the person we really wanted to stand with us early on was Senator Bernie Sanders. We saw him as someone who had never been an ordinary politician. If any public official understood our cause, we thought it would be him. The longest-serving independent in the U.S. Senate, Sanders grew up in a Jewish, working-class family in Brooklyn. Later, at the University of Chicago, he was an activist with radical civil rights groups like the Congress of Racial Equality (CORE) and the Student Nonviolent Coordinating Committee (SNCC). From the start, we were in contact with his team at More Perfect Union, and they promoted a lot of our videos. But again, we were surprised and disappointed that Sanders himself never came forward with his direct and open support of our campaign until after we won the vote.

Here's the takeaway from those lessons. Elected politicians that should have come through failed us. This only added to our belief that we wouldn't be tied to the traditional Democratic Party or to typical politicians. We saw how traditional unions were in the habit of endorsing candidates without even questioning them. **Instead, we decided not to endorse *any* political candidates.** It's even written in our constitution. Our belief is that the ALU is strictly here to serve our members and the larger working class, period.

For us, the takeaway was simple. High-profile individuals and influencers can play a part in calling positive attention to your movement and helping to build and expand your reach. After we won the vote, Cori Bush, Bernie Sanders, and Alexandria Ocasio-Cortez all lent their voices to our cause, and we were glad to have their contributions. They may have come to the party late, but they did come and were ultimately helpful.

But overall, organizers need to carefully consider opening

the door to parties or politicians. **We need to keep the door open to everyone, regardless of their voting records, beliefs, or backgrounds.** You don't want your movement to become primarily associated with any one group, because every worker needs to feel included regardless of their political affiliation.

And here's one last thought: **No politician is going to do more for you than what you can do for yourself by organizing inside the building.** What difference does it really make to workers to have a local politician in a suit and tie out there with them? How are they really going to make workers' lives better? Because the fact is, we're not just battling Amazon. In many ways, we're battling the established status quo of the two-party system. We're challenging their complicity every day. And that puts us on an even smaller island than we already are.

To Affiliate or Not to Affiliate

Earlier, I discussed how the ALU's victory was partly, in my opinion, due to our independence. But affiliating with larger unions is often a crucial decision in a campaign, and so I'd like to discuss it for a moment. Whether or not to affiliate, and when, is something that organizers will have to decide on a case-by-case basis. Every workplace is different, as are the demands and needs. It may be difficult to decide which road is best, and decisions can also change later down the line. The decision to go independent may not be right for every organization, but it absolutely was the right thing to do for us. Our independent ALU successfully won an election that traditional, big-name unions would not have been able to win.

We chose not to affiliate at the start of our movement for one simple reason: autonomy. We needed to do things *our* way, and we knew that a traditional union wouldn't support that. Imagine if we were under the Teamsters or SEIU and we said to them, "We want to have a barbecue at the bus stop and play rap music on a loudspeaker." Or, "We want our membership meetings to be outside over a bonfire. We don't want a hall setting." That goes against the same old tried-and-true template that they're used to, and it's very possible that they would've shut us down right then and there. Our creativity would be compromised, which could have seriously affected our confidence. And in my opinion, confidence is everything when it comes to organizing.

Going independent has its own challenges, though. You need to raise your own money, for one thing. Second, it can be daunting to feel like you don't have a known union name and infrastructure behind you; the lack of name recognition makes you have to work harder to be known, in addition to doing all the foundation building without outside help. Still, for us, being fully independent for the first three years of our existence was the right choice.

That changed in June 2024.

The International Brotherhood of Teamsters (IBT) had

been trying to get us to affiliate with them since the beginning. For years, they had targeted Amazon independently, making it a primary goal in their organizing efforts. In 2021, Teamsters delegates even voted to create an Amazon division at their planning convention. Every union collects union dues—so imagine if fifty-five hundred members pay $50 a month. That's $275,000 a month, or $3.3 million a year just from JFK8. Now, imagine if all six hundred Amazon buildings were to get unionized. That would be a huge win for the Teamsters.

Our victory at JFK8 was an opportunity too good for them to pass up. But each time they reached out to Chris, he would tell them no, since we had already decided to remain independent and to keep our own identity. But they kept coming back. Finally, they said, "What can we do to help convince you? Come to Washington, DC, and sit down with us."

We talked about it and came to the conclusion that it wouldn't hurt to meet with them. Since we were losing money at the time, we decided to go and hear them out.

Interestingly, Chris had been a Teamster years earlier, at age twenty-two, when he worked the graveyard shift at a grocery distribution warehouse in New Jersey. He didn't have a good experience with them back then. A manager used the N-word to him one day, and when he reported it to the Teamsters, they didn't do anything about it at all. So he was skeptical. None of us were sure they could offer us what we didn't already have—except money, of course. The constant fundraising was admittedly hard. We had a lot of bills to pay, and we knew some financial support could make a big difference to our movement.

Three ALU executive board officers and eight core organizers took the train down to Washington, DC, to the Teamsters' international headquarters. They put us up in a nice hotel around the corner, and when we got to the meeting, they had a whole PowerPoint presentation ready. Their group consisted of their board members and their president, Sean O'Brien. They talked about what they'd already been doing to help Amazon drivers—who are contracted through smaller third-party companies—organize in different states. Amazon had tried to say their drivers had nothing to do with those independent companies, but an NLRB judge disagreed and said that Amazon was, in fact, a joint employer. We knew the Teamsters had been doing some important organizing work for those workers.

But they'd never been able to crack the warehouses, even though they'd been trying for years. They openly acknowledged that we were the ones who opened that door and praised us. Then they jumped right into it. "We want you guys to affiliate." They said it straight, just like that. But we weren't sure. We had a back-and-forth discussion, trying to figure out how we might be able to get this done in a way that worked for everyone.

A few days later, Chris had a follow-up call with them, and we came to an agreement that the ALU would affiliate but retain full autonomy. What this meant was that we would still be able to organize the way we wanted to. It would be a partnership, where we would get strong support from the Teamsters locals and from other unions. A week or two later, we signed with them, and it was done. We became the ALU-IBT Local 1.

Is our affiliation a good thing? We hope so. Only time will tell.

It's true that affiliation has proven beneficial for unions at other large companies. Starbucks is affiliated with the SEIU, which has helped those workers do amazing things. They've unionized around five hundred stores since that first one voted yes in Buffalo, New York, in 2021.

In another case, Whole Foods workers affiliated with the UFCW, and in January 2025 workers at a Philadelphia store became the first to unionize, voting yes 130 to 100. Nationwide, at least ten other Whole Foods stores, which are owned by Amazon, have also started to organize, with the help of the UFCW. Apparently, Jeff Bezos dished out $13.7 billion for Whole Foods, yet he can't afford to pay workers there what in my opinion is a living wage!

Jennifer Bates at the Amazon facility at Bessemer, Alabama, says that affiliating with the RWDSU prior to their vote was a good move for them. She says there are many things they couldn't have accomplished without them. The union provided knowledge, legal help, finances, and on-the-ground organizing support, which they continue to offer even after the failed vote. Jennifer speaks highly of veteran, old-school RWDSU organizers like Randy Hadley, as well as Josh Brewer and Michael Foster ("Big Mike"), who worked in poultry plants for many years before becoming an RWDSU organizer. Each of these dedicated organizers has been there for Bessemer workers and taught them a lot. I think it's interesting that Jennifer is a minister, as are Josh and Mike. That common thread also probably ties them together and helps to create a positive leadership and organizing culture.

Every affiliation story is different.

Trader Joe's United is a lot like us. They started right after we did, and their leaders have often said that they were inspired by us. Today, they remain fully independent, "100 percent founded and powered by Trader Joe's workers" as they like to say. Since 2022, they've unionized four stores: in Hadley, Massachusetts; Minneapolis, Minnesota; Oakland, California; and Louisville, Kentucky, all without being affiliated with a bigger union.

Most of Trader Joe's United's financial support comes from employee dues, which are between 1 and 2 percent of gross wages once a contract is ratified. They also rely on selling union merchandise and donations from individual and community supporters. One thing that helped them a lot was a major ruling in May 2024, when a federal judge in California ordered Trader Joe's to pay more than one hundred thousand dollars in legal fees after it tried to sue them over trademark use. The union has also acknowledged receiving financial support from the UFCW, and possibly other unions.

How to Fight Counterattacks from Within

Internal counterattacks from your own people are the most loaded and, in many ways, the most difficult kinds of attacks to deal with. Three years ago, I would never have imagined that this book would need a section about attacks from within. Now, I know better. Infighting can derail even the most successful and ambitious movements. I can say from experience that every organizer needs to be prepared to face attacks from within.

After our victory, Chris and I received many accolades as president and vice president of the ALU. Our names were featured in major media outlets across the country. But the truth is, in every successful movement there will always be jealousy, egos, and petty rivalry. And sometimes those dynamics can unravel an entire organization.

In the summer of 2023, Connor Spence, who had formerly been our treasurer, decided to form an opposition group. He called it the ALU Democratic Reform Caucus. Michelle Valentin Nieves, the supporter who I mentioned earlier in the book, who I had personally recruited, made it her goal to replace me as vice president.

How did this all happen? What went wrong? To answer that question, I first need to start by discussing the backstory, which was never fully or truthfully explained in the media. In fact, there are members of the Reform Caucus who never even knew the full story until much, much later. So let me start from the beginning to offer a clearer picture of how trust issues, poor internal communication, and infighting have the potential to completely derail a successful movement.

The split within the ALU began with Connor and our constitution, which was a problem from the start.

The ALU was officially launched on April 20, 2021. For the next six months or so, until October 2021, we had an informal structure in place, which was expected under the circumstances. We were just starting out, scraping by. The constitution wasn't urgent. What was urgent was organizing. As our former lawyer Jeanne Mirer has explained in official proceedings, when unions are first formed, they're considered "nascent," which means they're given time to get themselves established and are usually run by an interim board. No one expects them to hold their first election for permanent officers until they've gotten off the ground.

Then, in October 2021, after our founding meeting, we asked Connor, who was serving as treasurer, to begin to draft a constitution, which he did. The way he went about it was to look at the constitutions of other unions and to put together a patchwork declaration based on those documents. The problem with that approach was that the other unions he looked at, like the United Electrical, Radio and Machine Workers (UE), had different circumstances than we did. For example, what he drafted gave the definition of "membership" as "anyone covered by the collective bargaining agreement." We didn't have a collective bargaining agreement yet, so that technically meant we had no members, which was a problem.

By May 2022, Jeanne had come on board as counsel to help our legal team. She said that the constitution drafted by Connor needed to be corrected and amended. We had several meetings with her that month to discuss and propose changes to different sections of the constitution. By early June, we were still working on the process when we suddenly had to shift our focus to the NLRB hearings taking place on Amazon's ULPs that came up during the election, and Amazon's two dozen objections to the election. Jeanne was busy with these more pressing legal issues, and honestly, we founders were more focused on organizing than anything else. We were putting time into the Albany campaign and the campaign at the other Staten Island Amazon facility. We weren't paying attention to things that we probably should have been more aware of.

The ALU still needed to be officially registered with the Department of Labor, and we hadn't yet filled out all our forms. That was when Connor took matters into his own hands. Sometime around the end of June 2022, he arranged to have a private meeting with DOL representatives behind our backs. Instead of filing our original constitution from October 2021, he filed an amended one; one that he had written himself and that he hadn't cleared with any of the other officers. In it, he stated that there would be an election for permanent officers within ninety days of the certification of the union. He didn't tell anyone that he made this change before filing the constitution, and it was never approved by the board.

It wasn't until November 2022, after the hearings on Amazon's objections were over, and the campaign in Albany was over, that the rest of us came back to the issue of finalizing the constitution. It was only then that we discovered what he'd done. We decided at that time to return to the original understanding that elections would happen only *after* we got a collective bargaining agreement with Amazon.

Basically, when Chris presented the constitution with the final changes in it, Connor and his supporters walked out of the room (later claiming that he was sick). He resigned as ALU treasurer and refused to participate in the final draft process. In our lawyer Jeanne's words, he had "improperly and unilaterally" replaced our founding constitution with his own revised version, which was never formally ratified by the board.

What did all this mean?

It meant that when our election was certified by a regional director in January 2023, it now triggered the need for an election, according to Connor's secretly amended version of the constitution. We were obligated to hold an election by April 2023 under a constitution no one on the board had agreed to. Connor was voted in with just 135 votes in a building with 5,000 workers, which wasn't the strongest endorsement. All of this was a huge distraction. What we needed was a bargaining contract, not an internal battle. We know for a fact that to this day, many workers in the building still don't really know or understand what happened. There were a lot of lies and misinformation that were fed to the press. In the confusion, we lost a good number of folks who had once been core supporters of our movement. In fact, we still don't believe that our former supporters knew about what Connor had done—that he had secretly met with the Department of Labor alone, without our lawyer, and filed his own constitution.

Our constitution was flawed and imperfect, but one thing that it clearly stated was that no one could go to the internet or to the media and disparage the union without first having a meeting with the recording secretary. Connor disregarded that. Instead, I understand he went straight to the media, creating turmoil, disinformation, and confusion. He even hired a lawyer, Arthur Schwartz, who got a judge to force that April 2023 election. We all filed objections to the results, and we won our appeal because fewer than 1 percent of workers in the building even participated in the vote. This is why we were granted another election to be held in December 2025, to redo the vote as a result of that appeal.

We could have and probably should have filed charges against Connor for violating our constitution but never did. Instead, we made the decision to try to protect the ALU's public image and to avoid the appearance of internal division or weakness. Maybe we could have avoided the mess we're in now if we had fought back more publicly. But we decided to take the high road and to keep our eyes on the prize. Maybe that was our biggest mistake.

If charges had been filed against him for violating a nondisparagement clause in the constitution, he would never have been eligible to run for an elected position. Should we have protected our burgeoning movement, even if it meant going public with these internal conflicts? I think so, looking back, but that's a decision that every organizer will have to make for themselves when faced with this kind of internal discord.

Those are the basic facts, as journalists would say; the who, what, when, where, and how. The deeper issue is why.

My fellow organizers and I believe that Connor's challenge came from a place of deep, and maybe even unconscious, insecurities. This is a white man who watched four powerful, independent Black men lead a movement composed of mostly people of color. Our initial board was majority Black and brown: Chris; me; Karen Ponce, who is Hispanic; and Jean-Michel Bowie, who is Black. (Connor is white.) Right from the start, there were cultural differences. It was a struggle for power from day one. I believe that he always had a hard time accepting and working through those issues with us. We saw him as a supporter and welcomed him into our movement. Our biggest mistake was that we trusted him and assumed that his intentions toward leaders of the union were good.

The people who left us to join his caucus are mostly white or white-presenting Latinos. Many of them are salts, the transplants who came to pitch in and play a temporary role. One of them, Brett Daniels, was sleeping on my couch when he first came from Arizona to join our movement. That's how much we trusted these people and welcomed them into our spaces. Brett had been an activist at the University of Arizona and later an organizer with the "Fight for $15." He reached out to Chris on social media when he saw our Covid walkout and moved to New York to get involved. We let everybody in.

But the question remains for their caucus: How are these outsiders going to relate to the mostly Black and brown workforce inside JFK8? How will they relate to young people coming from the Stapleton Houses, or the West Brighton Houses? Connor's first choices for an executive board were almost all white. That changed only after someone took him aside and challenged his decision, forcing him to rethink it.

Consistent support is hard to maintain in any movement, especially one as scrappy as ours. The losses at Albany and at Staten Island were tough to take. I understand why some workers watching from the sidelines may have questioned our choices. Some also questioned Chris's frequent travel. But what they don't understand is that it was his job. No union president sits in an office. They're doing events, conventions, and keynotes, supporting other movements and constantly raising money. When they say he should have stayed home more, it makes me laugh. It just proves that they have no idea what it takes to keep a movement like this going.

But what was most upsetting were the accusations put out in the national press. I feel they were clearly racial. They accused Chris of stealing money without proof and tried to imply that I had a troubled past, due to an altercation I had with an ex-girlfriend, a case where she never filed assault charges (the district attorney did), and which was later dismissed and expunged. I believe that these attacks were meant to destroy our credibility and our character. And because they came from within, it made it harder for some supporters to dismiss them. They carried more power and weight than anything Amazon could have ever said or done.

That's what I find most disturbing.

What does all this mean for other union campaigns and for organizers in other workplaces? I think it points to a larger problem within the labor movement, which is that we, as a society and as a movement, have not yet overcome basic power struggles along racial, class, and educational lines. Some continue to see Black men and women without fancy college degrees as not quite good enough to lead movements. I've heard plenty of stories about this. For example, some activists of color aren't offered the same honoraria for speaking engagements as their white counterparts. Some aren't given the same opportunities for advancement within union leadership. As founders of the ALU, we're not alone in feeling this dynamic. The question is, what can organizers do to combat these ingrained disparities and to move forward in solidarity?

I don't have the perfect answer to that. But here's what I do know: there will always be internal power dynamics and conflicts in any campaign and movement. At this very moment, there are members of the SEIU, the largest health care union in the country, who are trying to get rid of their own president. Unions fracture internally, at times; that's a fact. The key is to keep a close eye out as they develop and to always keep solidarity in mind as the most important goal as you work through issues together. Try to make sure that workers stay grounded in the collective intentions that you've all agreed on. How are you measuring success as a group? Talk about why you're doing what you're doing. Make sure that everyone has an opportunity to feel heard and to participate in the plan. We all want to feel like we have a full buy-in to the mission and like we're part of a solid and unified team.

The infighting weakened our movement in a profound way, to the point that the very survival of the ALU is currently even in question. We no longer have a united front, and there is deep disillusionment inside our building. A lot of people are completely turned off and don't want to hear anything about a union anymore. Morale is low and confusion is high. Amazon can easily take advantage of this lack of solidarity, and they have.

As founders, we understand that people have tried to change the narrative of how we got here. That's okay. *We* know how we got here. Someone might be able to take away my title, but there's no way they can take away my power. I never needed a title for that in the first place.

Now, going forward, we cofounders and our core supporters are in the process of trying to figure out what our involvement will be. There will be another election in December 2025, when we will hopefully put our own leadership back in place, generate renewed hope in the ALU, and finally get a contract.

Meanwhile, I'm still employed at JFK8 and am still actively advocating for workers. I'm a cofounder and organizer, still doing the work that I believe I was put on this earth to do. Here's what I think is the takeaway when it comes to internal attacks: Your power as an organizer and a leader shouldn't depend on any one election in any single building. The movement to improve the rights of workers is more than one campaign. It's much bigger, broader, and more powerful than any one individual. I've learned that it can be hard to see that sometimes, especially when you're deep in the weeds and your personal character and integrity are being challenged. But it's important to look beyond where you are at that moment, and to know that the power of the labor movement is a force that will not die.

Not Understanding the Big Picture

In the beginning, we thought affiliating with the International Brotherhood of Teamsters might help to resolve the internal split that was happening inside the ALU. Our position was that Teamsters could mediate between the two groups and help keep things under control while we figured out how to resolve our differences. Unfortunately, that never happened.

Once we realized that the Teamsters were unable to mediate a resolution, we decided that the best way to address the deeper issues at stake with Connor's attack and the ALU's internal split was to call them out, directly. We wrote a letter to the executive board of the IBT, where we spoke openly and honestly about racial dynamics and tensions within our movement.

Our letter said, in part:

"Since our affiliation there has been a clear and unfortunate divide with an apparent racial undertone. The original ALU leadership accepted folks from all different backgrounds." However, since July 2024 "none of the original organizers of the ALU have been allowed to be involved in Union activities, including the four Black founders who put their livelihoods and freedom at risk for the past five years . . . Many of the Black and Brown workers at JFK8 who have been working at JFK8 for five plus years or longer do not feel respected or represented . . . As founders and organizers," we continued, "we are expressing our concerns internally about the fact we are not integrated into the union." Our feeling was that true solidarity does not discriminate. Now, we wrote, it's "up to the IBT Leadership to exercise this beautiful solidarity in order to be successful."

This wasn't the first time the Teamsters had been called out for racism.

In early 2023, thirteen former employees, all Black and Latino, filed a racial discrimination lawsuit against Teamsters president Sean O'Brien for firing "more than a dozen people of color" and for making the Organizing Department "majority white." According to reporting in *The Guardian*, the Teamsters terminated more than 72 percent of the people of color on staff, while firing only about 28 percent of white employees. They then hired new staff who were more than 73 percent white. The lawsuit also claimed that O'Brien "publicly humiliated" the plaintiffs, who had "no history of negative performance reviews or disciplinary issues," calling them "bad apples" and "lazy."

In January 2024, the Teamsters paid $2.9 million to settle that lawsuit. We knew about this history, but because they had already been scrutinized by their own members, we thought they might change their ways and have a better understanding of how to approach Black and brown organizers.

Racism within the ranks isn't a problem only here in the United States. You can look around the world and see that there's almost no representation of Black or brown union leaders in other countries, either, except maybe in Latin America. Here in the United States, it wasn't until 2024 that April Verrett was elected the first Black international president of the SEIU in its 103-year history. The lack of women in leadership is also a huge problem. Out of twenty-seven leaders pictured on the Teamsters' website today, only two of them are women.

You only need to look at the December 2024 Amazon strike at JFK8 to see how infighting has weakened our movement. Although it may have looked like a lot of people participated because supporters from the Teamsters and other unions and activists arrived, only about fifteen workers from inside the building actually walked out. That's a red flag right there that you don't have strong internal support. For the Teamsters, the walkout still may have been a good thing, because it included drivers and warehouse workers from a total of nine facilities: five in California, one in Georgia, one in Illinois, and two in New York. Also, there were picket lines at maybe two hundred Amazon facilities total. But what may have been the right move for the IBT wasn't necessarily right for us at JFK8 as we continue to become more and more divided and fractured internally.

Why didn't this latest action do well? First, honestly, it was much too cold out there. It was like five degrees. We founders weren't involved in the planning at all, but if we had wanted to do something like that, we would have definitely done it in the spring or summer. We would've made a whole festival out of it, a celebration, like an ALU Field Day, giving out free stuff for workers while we strike. Second, it took place at around midnight, a few days before Christmas. That wasn't a good time. Third, you're telling workers to do something they've never done before at Amazon. Go on strike? You have to realize that this is totally new for them. What's more, two organizing groups inside the building were fighting and not putting their ideas and their power together. Of course you're going to have a low turnout. It was business as usual for Amazon, which felt no repercussions from that action whatsoever.

In early 2025, the four ALU founders along with our core team met with the Teamsters at their Local 210 offices on Staten Island. Some were there in person, others were on Zoom, along with the lawyers. There were ten of us in all. The meeting was long. We talked about possible strategies and plans. But what was disappointing, and surprising, was that not once did anyone address our letter. We later had another meeting, which was even worse. Again, no one thought it important even just to acknowledge what we had written. Some traditional, old-school unions do still have a problem recognizing their own racism. This experience gave us more proof of the unfortunate truth that these meetings only tore us further apart.

If, in the end, the ALU falls apart because of this infighting, conditions will only get worse for workers. Because now Amazon knows what they need to do. They'll just build an even better system of attack. So we need to think hard about our choices and what will happen in the coming months. As for us founders and original ALU supporters, we have our own plans. We're not stopping for anyone.

The Biggest Hurdle: Getting to a Contract

I've heard it said that back in the old days, organizing used to be the hardest part. That's not true anymore. Now the problem is getting to a contract. Our former lawyer Jeanne Mirer says we need to focus on asking one question:

"Where's Amazon?" We had an election. The workers voted yes. But where's Amazon? What are they hiding from? What are they afraid of? Every Amazon worker in America should be wearing a shirt that says, "Where's Amazon?"

Here's what organizers need to understand: The NLRB is never going to get anybody a contract. The NLRB is a tiny independent agency that is supposed to be staffed by five board members, and they have limited actual power. They can rule when an employee has been unfairly terminated, but they can't enforce any financial penalties for it. They can certify an election, but they can't force a contract. There are too many holes in the laws, and it's impossible for them to force companies like Amazon to the bargaining table. Also, the NLRB doesn't have any independent investigative power and can't bring charges against a company on its own. Only workers can do that. Even when it was friendly to us, the NLRB had no real power.

Big companies like Amazon don't care about penalties, and they know that U.S. federal labor laws have no teeth to enforce them anyway. After our win in April 2022, they filed twenty-five objections to the vote. They looked for any excuse, and it didn't matter how ridiculous. They said we bribed workers with marijuana, or harassed them, or intimidated them. We did give out weed, which wasn't a secret and wasn't illegal, even though it was portrayed that way. And we certainly didn't force anyone to vote on anything. The NLRB agreed to hearings over these absurd objections, which means our legal team had to sit in court for months listening to people telling lies on the stand.

In 2021, the House passed the PRO Act, which would have made labor laws stronger in several ways, including increasing penalties for employers who violate labor law, prohibiting mandatory captive audience meetings, challenging right-to-work laws, and streamlining the process of getting to first contracts and collective bargaining through mediation and arbitration, among other important measures. It was introduced by two Democrats, Representative Bobby Scott from Virginia and Senator Patty Murray from Washington, but it was voted down in the Senate.

By the same token, NLRB general counsel Jennifer Abruzzo tried to make some important changes under President Biden. She put new rules in place on captive audience meetings in April 2022, finally acknowledging that they're coercive. But Abruzzo was fired by Donald Trump the *same night* that Whole Foods Philadelphia voted to unionize. A week after taking office as president, he also illegally fired NLRB chair Gwynne Wilcox, the first Black woman to serve in the board's entire ninety-year history. (Wilcox was later reinstated by a federal judge who noted in his ruling that the president is not a king, though the NLRB remains severely disenfranchised.)

Another of our former lawyers, Seth Goldstein, talks about how companies like Amazon seem to hire huge pro-company law firms like Morgan Lewis or Ogletree, paying them millions of dollars to delay coming to the table. There's a tactic they use, for example, called "surface bargaining," which basically means they're going to pretend they're bargaining when they're really not. They'll put in proposals that are maybe 95 percent okay, but that also contain "poison pills" where 5 percent of the contract is problematic. That 5 percent will try to do something like throw employees out of their 401(k) plans, which they know is unacceptable. So the whole strategy is just to delay.

Seth once put it very bluntly. He said, "You can't go into these rooms and treat these people like honorable gentlemen. Because they're not honorable gentlemen. They're there for one purpose. To destroy you."

But there have been some victories along the way.

The Cemex decision of August 2023 was an NLRB ruling that required employers to automatically recognize unions if most employees signed authorization cards. There are some labor leaders who are hopeful about this ruling and think it could force companies to the table. That same year, Trader Joe's United became the first union to file a bargaining order under the new Cemex framework, but a hearing on that case is still pending.

Another victory came in November 2024, when the NLRB ruled that Amazon violated federal law by requiring attendance at anti-union captive audience meetings. They made it clear that such meetings could be held only if attendance was voluntary "with no adverse consequences for failure to attend, and that no attendance records of the meeting will be kept."

A few months later, in February 2025, a judge said that Amazon illegally enforced its UPT policy to penalize workers who were legally engaged in walkouts and strikes. Another huge legal win. At least on paper. Still, we all know that none of these rulings can really be enforced. Which means, basically, our labor laws are failing us. It's illegal to fire someone for organizing a union; Americans have a federally protected right to unionize. Yet illegal firings happen in 30 percent of union campaigns.

Just look at my friend and cofounder Gerald Bryson's case. He was illegally fired in 2020 for leading two safety protests, which workers have the right to do when they're forced to work in unsafe conditions, during Covid. Gerald had a 10J, meaning a Section 10(j) injunction filed by the NLRB, which is even higher than a ULP. It said Amazon needed to temporarily reinstate him to his job while the case was being investigated. He then won his case against Amazon for wrongful termination. It was such a big deal that Amazon was ordered to read Gerald's case to workers in the break room, which was huge for our campaign.

But Amazon never offered Gerald his job back. That's why the NLRB sued Amazon in 2022, saying they had to. (The NLRB case is still pending.) To this day, he's still going back and forth in court. It's been more than five years and he has never received any back pay or compensation. The fact that Amazon can continue to drag this out when the NLRB has already ruled in his favor is astounding. So again, the laws are failing us.

What can organizers do in the face of weak labor laws? I'll tell you what will work. As always, there is power in numbers. To truly make progress, it will take a wide cross section of people—workers, consumers, lawmakers, and advocates—engaging in a wide variety of direct-action approaches to force companies to recognize unions and their demands. Even the most solid and powerful group of organizers in a building simply can't do it alone. The only way we're going to get to a contract is by using the methods outlined above to help change the wider culture. Basic workers' rights need to be seen as a given, as basic human rights.

And I believe the tide is shifting.

There is growing anger among American workers that's undeniable. From 2021 to 2022 the NLRB saw a 53 percent increase in union petitions. In 2022, representation petitions increased by 60 percent. There have been massive organizing waves in recent years, at companies like Starbucks, Microsoft, Google, Trader Joe's, and Apple, and across small businesses nationwide.

The workers are the ones creating and leading us on a path forward, not the legislators or the politicians. We need much more of this kind of collective action, and much less focus on the courts and federal agencies. Getting to a contract is always going to be about alliances between workers and consumers, about consumers using their buying power to support workers and their rights. It's always going to be about pressuring politicians to get their hands out of big corporate pockets and to be on the right side of history. We need to remind ourselves that in the end, it wasn't the NLRB that won the election at JFK8. It was us. Workers organizing creates undeniable, powerful energy that can't be stopped. It's historical. Labor unions aren't going anywhere.

A Larger Movement

Companies like Amazon and Trader Joe's followed Trump's lead in his early months of office, joining him in arguing that the NLRB is unconstitutional. Their goal is to dismantle it completely as a protector of workers' rights. They want a world where no laws get in the way of big business and what they see as their inherent right to enjoy unlimited profit. But something happened along the way at Trader Joe's that made me hopeful.

When the company announced their agreement with Trump's goals, the workers at the Essex Crossing Trader Joe's in Lower Manhattan weren't trying to hear it. So they walked out. More importantly, they asked for support from their customers—and they got it! New Yorkers didn't have any problem at all throwing their weight in the battle and joining in the protest. Union members posted the phone numbers of Trader Joe's corporate leadership in Monrovia, California, on Instagram, asking people to call them and voice their dissatisfaction. And that's exactly what they did. Customers flooded the phone lines of Trader Joe's CEO Bryan Palbaum, vice CEO Jon Basalone, and deputy general counsel Nancy Inesta.

There was even a sample script they could follow. It said, "More and more customers like myself are willing to stop shopping at Trader Joe's. Your actions are not aligning with your values and we don't want to give money to a company that doesn't treat its workers fairly." And guess what? The campaign worked. The company abandoned its legal challenge to the NLRB because of direct action and consumer support.

Traditional methods continue to work, too. What about the Kellogg's workers who went on strike in October 2021? About fourteen hundred people left their jobs for three months, walking out of four buildings in Michigan, Nebraska, Pennsylvania, and Tennessee. That worked, too. After eleven weeks, the company caved and gave them a five-year contract.

Costco has a reputation for positive worker relations and a low turnover rate. But behind closed doors, the truth is that they didn't come to a contract agreement with the union easily. The company held out and delayed negotiations for as long as possible, not showing up to meetings and giving workers a hard time. It wasn't until the threat of a strike that they finally came to a tentative collective bargaining agreement. Sometimes what works is customer support and boycotts. Sometimes it might take a walkout. Sometimes what's needed is both. We also need much stronger laws, but it will take pressure on the ground to get those. We have to be able to fight on all these fronts. A group of workers in a single building can get only so far alone, no matter how strong they may be. Without all these other strategies and actions, as well as comprehensive legal, political, cultural, and societal support systems, we'll continue to be limited in the progress we make.

Let me give an example of what I mean by our collective power.

Our former attorney Jeanne Mirer was involved with the Hot and Crusty bakery campaign of 2012 here in New York, where they had massive community involvement. They won their union election and got a contract with the help of activists and community members from Occupy Wall Street as supporters. That community picketed for fifty-two days, 24-7, and wouldn't let the restaurant shut down. The landlord couldn't rent it. Eventually, the workers got a contract. There's even a documentary about it. It's called *The Hand That Feeds*. This situation is different from Amazon, of course. Hot and Crusty is a small shop with thirty to one hundred workers. We can't compare it to organizing six thousand people in a building at a multinational corporation. But it does show the power of workers and communities united and the success of massive actions that build on this collective strength.

We live in a time of extremes. Wealth inequality has never been greater. The gap between those who have more than they can ever hope to spend in a lifetime and those hoping to stay housed and fed until their next paycheck is increasing every day. But there has also been a shift in recent years. The rights of undervalued workers are now being recognized more and more, because we're insisting on it. We're fighting back against job insecurity, racial discrimination, low wages, and unreasonable workplace quotas.

We are at a pivotal time in history. Workers need to recognize fully the power they have and know how to leverage it. There will be a spark in the labor movement, and it will become a fire. We're not there yet. But it's coming.

One recent victory came in April 2025, when a regional NLRB in San Francisco ruled that Amazon was in violation of federal law under the Cemex ruling and ordered the company to begin bargaining in good faith with more than one hundred workers at the DCK6 warehouse there. The Teamsters' legal teams are arguing that Amazon is violating this order at eight locations across the country. We'll see what happens next, but we all know it will be a rough road ahead given Trump's hostility to labor.

The most important thing to remember is that this unionization process is a long one. There are a lot of things that go on behind the scenes. **This is a marathon, not a sprint.** How can organizers play the long game without getting distracted, disillusioned, or burnt out? How can we stay positive when the situation looks so bad? I believe that the key is staying connected—to one another as members and supporters of the union, to those who inspire and fuel us, and to ourselves and our own core beliefs.

On April 10, 2025, I received a text message at around 1:00 a.m. It was from a coworker asking if I was awake. As I've mentioned a few times, I'm pretty much always awake throughout the night, but this time I was asleep and the text woke me.

"Wussup," I answered. She sent me a screenshot from the Citizen app saying that someone had been run over by an Amazon truck at JFK8 and killed. At the time, we didn't know who the person was. From that point on, the texts kept coming.

"Hey u up," came another one at 2:48 a.m. telling me that they'd sent everyone in the building home. Later that morning Amazon told us that there would be a four-hour delayed opening while the police were investigating the incident. (They later decided to keep the building closed for the entire day.) What was shocking was that Amazon's message didn't mention anything about anyone dying—much less the fact that it was a fellow worker who was killed.

I sent a WhatsApp group chat message to the other founders and to all our core organizers asking everyone to try to get as much information as they could.

Eventually, we found out that the worker's name was Leony Salcedo-Chevalier. He was a delivery driver from Perth Amboy, New Jersey, which is twenty minutes away from my hometown of Piscataway. We also found out that he was thirty-four and had two daughters. News reports later said he was born in Santiago, Dominican Republic.

I couldn't imagine what it would feel like to get a phone

call saying someone in my family had died at work. What made the situation even worse was that in the news reports Amazon kept calling him a "third-party employee." They repeated this over and over because, of course, they didn't want to be held accountable for his death.

My coworkers were outraged and were speaking up on the Voice of Associates board. Even though Amazon said that night-shift workers were still supposed to show up for work, when I drove out to demand that the building stay closed, I saw that the parking lot was damn near empty. I haven't seen it that empty since Covid. Workers were frustrated and angry and many of them decided not to show up. Later I found out that any worker that wanted to stay home that day was able to do so without having any of their UPT deducted, which was a victory, but Amazon never announced this or made their concession public.

This tragedy reminded me of the importance of staying in constant communication with one another. Workers are the ones who give me the energy to keep going. Because they're not going to let up. They're going to keep asking, "Okay, we have a union now, so what's going on? Why aren't any changes being made yet? How is our situation better now that we have the union?"

Some of them are under the impression that after you win, that's it. Everything improves just like that. They don't understand that there's a long appeal process, a court process, and that Amazon is going to drag things out for as long as possible to avoid bargaining. As organizers, we understand this, and we know that the courts take a long time to get things done. Our job is to break that down for other workers. **Send out text messages and emails, providing updates about the appeal trial. Communicate exactly what's happening every step of the way.**

We make sure that we have a whole checklist of people who need to get updates, starting with those who first signed authorization cards. We send out a mass text with key information, so they all get it. We show them that we're being transparent about the whole process because transparency is key. We also have Zoom meetings, or town halls, on a regular basis with workers from all over the United States. It's not just JFK8 that we're focused on, but other warehouses across the country.

We need to keep going, keep fighting, keep speaking out, and keep educating. I believe that ultimately being a leader and organizing doesn't boil down to just a vote. It's bigger than that. Organizing is a belief system and a way of life.

Another way to stay positive is by giving back. Chris and I have met with elementary, middle, and high school students. We've visited classrooms in Brooklyn and Jersey City, where we were the keynote speakers for Career Day. We've talked about organizing with a roomful of 150 seventh and eighth graders. The work of educating is so important because if we can talk to kids when they're young, then they can help to spread that knowledge when they get older and are inside their own workplaces.

Chris's cousin is a college student at William Paterson

University in New Jersey, and she said her class spent a whole semester learning about the ALU, which is so special. Once, a group of Black kids from Mississippi traveled all the way to New York to meet with us. We spoke with them at the People's Forum in New York City. Labor professors have invited us to speak to their classes. I was on a Zoom for a class at the University of Toronto. They put the video screen up on a giant projector in an auditorium.

We're part of American history now.

This moment has the potential to be a real turning point, but for that to happen, I believe workers need to continue to realize their true worth. The struggle is much deeper than just fighting for a union. **We're fighting for our humanity.**

A New American Labor Party

Flashback to early 2024. The four of us founders were all at the ALU office, about five minutes away from JFK8. We had just finished a meeting, and we were sitting in Gerald's car in the parking lot, smoking. At that moment, the ideas were just flying around. We all knew Trump was going to win the election. We were also shocked by how, on social media, there were these "Blacks for Trump" groups. We were just completely baffled. We knew a lot of Amazon workers supported him, too. For one thing, many of them don't follow any kind of actual news. They just scroll down Instagram, look somewhere like the Shade Room, and take in whatever's there. We knew Trump had the momentum, and it was scary.

Suddenly, Chris was just like, "You know what? We should just start a Labor Party." It wasn't the first time he'd mentioned this. But on this day, we all felt it more strongly. The Democratic Party was not serving workers, and the laws weren't in our favor. That's how it started.

Today, the four of us cofounders are in the process of forming a new Labor Party that fights strictly for workers. We already have a website, thelaborpartyus.com, and an Instagram page @thelaborpartyusa, and we're starting the process of getting other activists and organizers involved. Our plan is to build over the next few years, slowly and steadily, taking our time with foundation building. We've already outlined some powerful policies and are continuing to build internally ahead of our official launch. Folks who want to support this effort can sign up for updates or DM/email us directly.

The U.S. Labor Party was formed in 1973 and dissolved just six short years later in 1979. The Green Party, which is still active, is great. We've met with both Jill Stein and Cornel West. We support them, although we don't give official endorsements to any candidates. But we also believe that our Labor Party needs fresh faces and younger people leading the movement. The way we see it, it's another small idea that could turn into a huge movement. And who is better to do this than the people who formed the first union for Amazon?

Just as we started ALU, we're going to just go out there and see what we can do. The hard truth is that the two-party system we have is not working. It's great that Joe Biden came out to support the United Auto Workers in September 2023, making him the first sitting U.S. president to join workers on a picket line. That was a nice photo opportunity, and it looked good. But what did it really do for workers? And we certainly can't expect huge labor victories under the Trump administration. The best thing we can do is get back to our grassroots efforts and organize in this fresh new way.

I've said it before, and I'll end with these words: For me, organizing is about inspiring young people to reach beyond wherever they are and to have the courage to go for what they want in life. This book is a handbook for a workers' revolution. My hope is that my story and these lessons will give us an even bigger voice and platform to reach as many people as possible. The goal is not only to continue to educate one another, first with those of us who are in the movement, but also to inspire people outside the movement, people who may be totally disconnected from us and have no idea about the rights they already have as workers, not to mention the enormous impact that their voice could make, if they choose to use it. Because the truth is, the workers' revolution is bigger than any one group of workers and it's bigger than any one company. A workers' revolution is a revolution for humanity.

Glossary of Terms

Ambassador: An Amazon employee who trains new workers

Authorization cards: Cards with a worker's full name and signature, which means that they want to be represented by a union

Captive audience meetings: Mandatory meetings where workers must listen to anti-labor speeches designed to force workers to vote no on unions

Count: An Amazon department that keeps track of inventory and investigates discrepancies

JFK8: The largest Amazon fulfillment center in New York state and one of four Amazon buildings on Staten Island. The others are LDJ5, a sorting center for merchandise; DYY6, a delivery station; and DYX2, a distribution center, which was closed in 2023.

Picker: An Amazon worker who retrieves items from bins based on customer orders. Pick makes up one of six main departments at JFK8, which include: Receive, Stow, Count, Pick, Pack, and Ship Dock.

Process assistant (PA): A supervisory role at Amazon

Protecting the Right to Organize (PRO) Act: Legislation aimed at strengthening the rights of employees to unionize and collectively bargain in the United States. Introduced in 2019, it has passed in the House of Representatives but stalled in the Senate.

Salts: Union organizers who typically come from other cities and states to help kick-start campaigns

Time off task (TOT): The amount of time an Amazon warehouse worker spends not actively scanning packages or engaging with warehouse systems, tracked automatically through scanners and software

Unfair Labor Practice (ULP) complaint: A violation of workers' rights under federal labor law. ULPs can be filed by workers, unions, or employers when someone interferes with protected rights.

Union drive: The beginning of a campaign when workers officially attempt to gain support from employees to create a union

Unpaid time off (UPT): Time that Amazon workers can use, if available, to take off work without being penalized

Warehouse Worker Protection Act: A New York state law designed to protect warehouse workers from dangerous productivity quotas that can violate their rights and threaten their health

Connect to Additional Resources

Derrick Palmer
https://www.instagram.com/true__toself/

Christian Smalls
https://www.instagram.com/chris.smalls_/

Gerald Bryson
https://www.instagram.com/universal__son/

Jordan Flowers
https://www.instagram.com/jayytcoew23/

Tristan Dutchin
https://www.instagram.com/simba_lion_tristan/

The Amazon Labor Union (ALU)
https://www.amazonlaborunion.org/
https://www.instagram.com/amazonlaborunion/
https://www.instagram.com/amazonlaborunion_local1/

The Congress of Essential Workers (TCOEW)
https://x.com/tcoew
https://www.instagram.com/tcoew/

The U.S. Labor Party
https://www.thelaborpartyus.com/
https://www.instagram.com/thelaborpartyusa/

• • •

All Workers Militant Front (PAME)
https://pamehellas.gr/what-is-pame

American Federation of Labor and Congress of Industrial Organizations (AFL-CIO)
https://aflcio.org/

American Federation of Teachers
https://www.aft.org/

Apple Retail Union
https://appleretailunion.org/

Carolina Amazonians United for Solidarity and Empowerment (CAUSE)
https://amazoncause.com/

Communications Workers of America Union (CWA)
https://cwa-union.org/

International Brotherhood of Teamsters (IBT)
https://teamster.org/

International Longshoremen's Association
https://ilaunion.org/

Make the Road New York
https://maketheroadny.org/

More Perfect Union
https://perfectunion.us/

National Labor Relations Board (NLRB)
https://www.nlrb.gov/

Occupational Safety and Health Administration (OSHA)
https://www.osha.gov/

Poor People's Campaign
https://www.poorpeoplescampaign.org/

Retail, Wholesale and Department Store Union (RWDSU)
https://www.rwdsu.org/

Service Employees International Union (SEIU)
https://seiu.org/

Socialist Alternative
https://www.socialistalternative.org/

Starbucks Workers United
https://sbworkersunited.org/

Trader Joe's United
https://traderjoesunited.org/

Unifor
https://www.unifor.org/

***Union* (Film)**
https://www.unionthefilm.com/

Unite Here!
https://unitehere.org/

United Food and Commercial Workers International Union (UFCW)
https://www.ufcw.org/

U.S. Department of Labor
https://dol.gov

Acknowledgments

I want to thank my mother, Carol Boulden, for being my number-one supporter no matter what. I've always been a free spirit, living in the moment; her grounding is what has kept me balanced. I grew up in a single-parent household and we often struggled financially, but she always found a way to overcome those challenges. She had a "no excuses" mindset that has made me the man I am today. When I have children, I hope to teach them that same mindset.

I also want to give a special shout-out to my uncle and aunt, James Thomas and Gayle Bussey, who took care of me at an early age. At their house in Roselle, New Jersey, I learned how to rake leaves, shovel snow, and wash cars, which was huge for me at the age of ten. I will always remember watching the New York Giants and Knicks games with Uncle James, who sat in his favorite chair drinking his Old Milwaukee beer. I loved those days, as well as watching tennis games with Aunt Gayle: Venus and Serena Williams, Pete Sampras and Andre Agassi.

I want to thank Soeke Lumor, my childhood best friend, who's been like a brother ever since we met in third grade at Grandview Elementary School in Piscataway. His parents, Seth and Cynthia, treated me like family and made sure their house was always like my second home.

Special shout-outs to my siblings, Terrell Irving, Anthony Felix, Tierra Palmer, and Jaiden Palmer, for always supporting my journey. I also want to acknowledge my aunt Linda and uncle John for their support throughout my journey.

I'm grateful for my brother and comrade Chris Smalls, who has always looked out for me. Just being around him has taught me so much. He's bold and charismatic, and he never gives up. We stood side by side throughout this journey as founders of the Congress of Essential Workers and the Amazon Labor Union. I'm looking forward to what else we can accomplish in the labor movement and beyond. That's my brother for life.

I want to give another special shout-out to Ashley Cen for always being by my side. I have so much admiration for her, working full-time and raising three children on her own. She's not only intelligent and book-smart; she's also street-smart and bold. I feel so grateful to have her in my life.

Thank you to my guy Tristan Dutchin, a.k.a. Tristan Lion, one of the most generous and kindhearted people I've ever met. His spiritual connection with the ancestors is reflected in his music and I'm proud to call him my brother.

Thank you to my brothers Jordan Flowers and Gerald Bryson, who were there for me through some dark times. I will always be appreciative of that. One day we're chilling in the house watching sports and the next we're organizing at the bus stop at JFK8. I look forward to seeing what we do next.

Thank you to Kristal Brent Zook, the cowriter of this book and an amazing person to work with. I knew right away that she was the one I wanted on this project. Her attention to detail and understanding of my story made all the difference. Who knows, we might work together again one day on another book!

My literary agents Laura Nolan and Jennifer Gates from Aevitas Creative Management have been nothing but supportive and kind throughout this journey. I'm extremely grateful for how they believed in my vision and stuck with me.

Thank you to Jackson Howard, senior editor at Farrar, Straus and Giroux, who understood and supported my vision from the start. He knew how important it was for workers across the world to hear my story and to have a guide like this one.

Finally, I want to acknowledge all the Amazon workers around the world, especially the ones at JFK8 in Staten Island, New York, and EWR4 in Robbinsville, New Jersey. I've met so many great people during my ten-year run at this company. My hope is that every one of you recognizes your worth and understands that this company doesn't thrive without us.

A Note About the Author

Derrick Palmer is the cofounder of the Amazon Labor Union, which, in 2022, successfully unionized an Amazon warehouse for the first time in the company's history. The same year, he and his union cofounder Christian Smalls were honored with placement on *Time*'s 100 Most Influential People list and as one of the Dynamic Duos on *Ebony*'s Power 100 list. He continues to work at the Amazon JFK8 warehouse in Staten Island, New York, where he lives.